Firefly

Ashley's Light

Jane Ashe

Firefly: Ashley's Light
Copyright © 2023 by Jane Ashe

All rights reserved. This book or any portion thereof may not be reproduced or used in any manner whatsoever without the express written permission of the publisher, except for the use of brief quotations in a book review.

Printed in the United States of America.

Luminare Press
442 Charnelton St.
Eugene, OR 97401
www.luminarepress.com

LCCN: 2022923708
ISBN: 979-8-88679-059-7

To Anna and Andrew

The highest knowledge is to know you are surrounded by mystery.

—Albert Schweitzer[1]

Contents

Preface ix

Part I
Opening 3

Part II
The Search 31

Part III
Beyond 59

Acknowledgments 131
Bibliography 132
Endnotes 133

Preface

Because *Firefly* is a story about the search for my daughter (literally and spiritually), I think it is important to let you know where I am coming from spiritually. I honor and embrace all paths that lead to love and peace. When referring to the Sacred, Divine, or Holy, I use the word God. I believe that God is always present, and when we suffer, God suffers with us.

Firefly

Ashley's Light

FIREFLY
(A SONG)

> A little light is going by.
> Is going up to see the sky,
> A little light with wings.
>
> I never could have thought of it.
> To have a little bug all lit
> And made to go on wings.
>
> —Elizabeth Madox Roberts[2]

PART I
Opening

THE PACT

I remember it as though it were yesterday, although we shook hands on it twenty-five years ago.

It was a crisp, sunny day in September when my daughter Ashley was home for the weekend during her junior year at University of Washington. We were upstairs in her attic bedroom when we made a pact and shook on it: Whoever died first would do everything we could, if it were allowable in our new location, to demonstrate that there was, in fact, life after death.

The death pact was my idea, but Ashley was game. I had been reading a novel where the author offered an autobiographical note about an occurrence after her husband's funeral. It was winter, and she decided to take a walk outside in her garden. The leaves on the trees were gone, and the foliage on the bushes folded in tight for the season. However, passing by her favorite rosebush, she was surprised to see it was in full bloom. Lovely red roses opened through green leaves when before the funeral they were not. Her husband had known this was her favorite rosebush.

I told Ashley about the author's note. We thought it was cool and agreed we would try to do something similar to let the other one know we were still around when the occasion arose. I assured my twenty-year-old daughter I was certain to go first but still wanted to make an agreement.

I didn't think I was going to die first but didn't allow myself to believe it, and here's why. When I was seventeen, circa 1965, my mother died after fighting cancer for fourteen years. When I came home after the funeral, I sat on my white, nubby bedspread, partially glanced out the window facing the street, and told my mom in no uncertain terms not to show herself by sitting on my bed or anywhere else. I didn't want any of that kind of stuff. I told Mom to stay put where she was and not make any surprise appearances. I knew she loved me so much that she would appear if permitted. No way did I want that.

The next day, I thought how strange it was that I would shut myself in my room to make that kind of announcement. I had no experience with the supernatural, but I knew if she could, Mom would make it known she was still around.

All that said, thereafter I had an infrequent but recurring dream of standing over my mom's coffin, looking at her all dressed up in her gray tailored suit, makeup on and hair styled like she used to wear it, with nobody home inside. It was creepy. This dream floated in from time to time as years went by. When it appeared, I'd feel distressed, thinking, *Oh no, not this again.*

One day in 1976, when my kids were young (Ashley three, Anna six), I woke up from the same dreaded dream. This time I was surprised to see another coffin about forty-five degrees off to the side of Mom's. Curious, I walked over to it, standing back and leaning slightly. I was unable to determine who if anyone was inside, and I woke up confused. The dream with two coffins occurred again and again. With each dream, I got closer, and the image became slightly more discernible. I could tell there was a person inside who did not take up the whole length of the space—neither a child nor an adult, somewhere in between. The face never became clear, but I awoke knowing it was Ashley, not her sister, Anna, or anyone else. Upset by the content of the dream and the final recognition that it was Ashley, I tried to put it out of my mind.

My friend Janet had two girls the same ages as mine. We raised them side by side as neighbors and friends. During this time, due to parallel life transitions, our families were living together like a sorority—two big girls and four little girls. In the hope of ridding the images and thoughts from my mind, I decided to tell Janet. I thought that by voicing my fear out loud, the sense of foreboding would vanish and I could be free of it. I could say to myself, *It's just a dream. Don't worry about it. It will go away.*

One afternoon when the kids were playing outside, I said to Janet, "I think Ashley is going to die—not now but later when she's older, not quite an adult." I told her about the dreams and how they kept coming back and that I was terribly, horribly scared.

She listened intently, looked me straight in the eyes, and said adamantly, "Jane, Ashley is *not* going to die."

I replied, "Are you sure?"

"*Yes*, I'm sure!" she said.

Relieved, because Janet was a wise and trusted friend, I chose to believe her. Thank God I told her. Now I could parent Ashley normally, letting go of the fear of her early death. Maybe the thought would disappear altogether. It did, however, travel to the back of my mind, surfacing to the front every now and then. I'd manage to beat it down, reminding myself of Janet's forceful assurance that Ashley was not going to die. I'd reassure myself that if Ashley could make it to twenty-one, a bona fide legal adult, the dreams would become null and void because she would no longer be between a child and an adult. It was like a fairytale. I was so relieved when Ashley turned twenty-one, thinking, *Maybe it was just a dream after all.*

Opening

CHILDHOOD

Ashley and her third-grade classmates at Saint Joseph's Catholic School excitedly rehearsed their parts as fireflies for the Christmas play. The idea of fireflies in a Christmas play was a new and imaginative concept for me. A letter from her teacher informed the parents that all Ashley and her fellow students would need for their costumes was a flashlight. Their uniforms were navy-blue pants and sweaters, dark enough for a firefly body. The kids' roles consisted of running around in a circle with flashlights turned on in the corner of the stage, off to the side of the sheep and goats. For a Christmas play, I never could have thought of it.

As soon as I mentioned the firefly concept to Jane Langer, my new friend at work, she smiled with her twinkly eyes and remarked, "Oh, I have a poem about fireflies. I'll bring it to work tomorrow." She brought it and read it to me with even twinklier eyes, if that's possible. After Jane's reading, I often thought of Ashley as a firefly. Since she flew off the planet, she continued to buzz around, occasionally flashing her light where sometimes I could see it.

ANNA WAS BORN IN 1970, A BEAUTIFUL BABY GIRL WITH silky, light-brown hair, fair skin, and green eyes. Ashley, born in 1973, had curly, black hair and an olive complexion.

Firefly

Both eventually stood under five foot two—short in stature and long in soul. Writings and a poem by Anne Cameron capture the common denominator of them both. Until I read Cameron's *Daughters of Copper Woman*, I had no words.

Opening

Children of Happiness are not like ordinary children. They are usually girls, but sometimes little boys are born with the signs. You can tell one of the Children of Happiness by the way it is different. A Child of Happiness always seems like an old soul living in a new body, and her face is very serious until she smiles, and then the sun lights up the world. You look at the eyes of a Child of Happiness and you know the child knows everything that is truly important. . . .

THE CHILDREN OF HAPPINESS
>They are to be cherished and protected,
>even at the risk of your life.
>They will know sadness, but will overcome it.
>They will know alienation
>for they see past and through this reality.
>They will Endure where others cannot.
>They will Survive where others cannot.
>They will know love even when it is not shown
>>to them.
>They spend their lives trying to
>>Communicate
>the love they know.
>—Anne Cameron, *Daughters of Copper Woman*[3]

Firefly

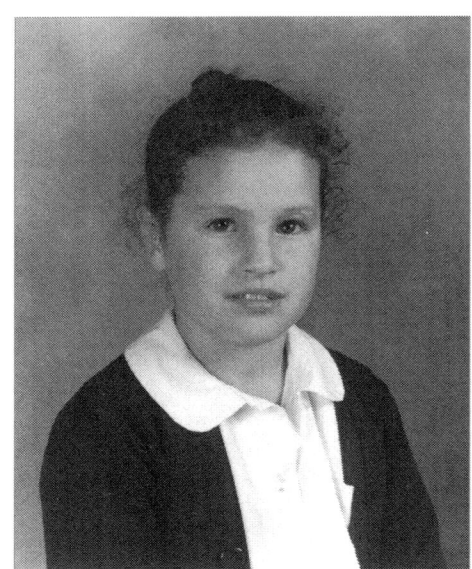

Saint Joseph's Elementary

Opening

ALTHOUGH CAUCASIAN, ASHLEY SAID THAT PEOPLE WHO'D just met her thought she was the nationality that they were whether African American, Italian, Vietnamese, Chinese, Japanese, Korean, or Indian. She said this combination of physical traits was helpful in relating to all kinds of people and groups. In truth, she was mostly Irish and Italian.

EARLY ONE MORNING, FOUR-YEAR OLD ASHLEY SAT DOWN in her child-sized pine rocking chair and announced, "There will only be one day that is today. Tomorrow it will be gone. We need to see all that is around us. Do you see what I mean?" She was looking at the shape of the chair and the sun coming in through the dining room window.

ASHLEY ENTERED PRESCHOOL, AND ANNA BEGAN FIRST grade when their dad Ralph married Marlys, who had a young son Andrew from her prior marriage. Marlys became the girls' other mother, and Andrew became their brother. The siblings were all very close. The girls traveled back and forth between the two houses every other week.

Firefly

SCHEDULED TO MEET Ms. D. FOR THE PARENT-TEACHER conference at Stevens Elementary School, I looked forward to a sweet conversation about what a good kid Ashley was and how well she participated in class. However, Ms. D. told me, "Ashley is causing problems for me and the class. So many of the children quarrel over who will get to sit by her that it is making it difficult to control the environment for learning." Although a seasoned kindergarten teacher, Ms. D. was frustrated and asked for my thoughts. She seemed to think that Ashley was manipulating the kids by telling one "you can sit by me today" and another "you can sit by me tomorrow."

Surprised to hear about this situation, I laughed as I told Ms. D., "Her solution is exactly how her dad and I solved joint custody in our divorce: one week with Dad and the next week with Mom."

Ms. D. laughed. The ball was left in her court, and she concluded that Ashley was not being manipulative, just trying to solve a problem based on her experience.

In the fourth grade, Ashley said, "I don't know how other kids whose parents are home when they return from school can deal with having them there." I worked full time, and she

Opening

and Anna came home after school when they were old enough and took care of themselves. During this time, Ashley liked to relax, have a snack, and, along with other projects, assemble a bank business in a gray, metal file cardbox where she drew and listed characteristics of bank members. She did this for hours on end. During this time, Anna and Ashley also wrote poetry under the tutelage of a writer friend.

"The Cold Butterfly"
By Ashley Palumbo
One evening in December as snow lightly drifted
to the ground, a small tree stood in the forest.
Suddenly he heard a noise: Flitter, Flitter, Flitter
Flitter. I saw the colorful thing it was a butterfly.
It came to me and said, "I am very cold do you
know where I could stay?" So I said, "there is a
nice warm hole in me that you could stay in." So the
little butterfly stayed in my hole.
The End
1982

ANNA WAS HER STEADY COMFORT AND GUIDE AS THEY traveled back and forth between my house and Ralph and Marlys's house every other week. They were extremely close. When home, they played together without asking friends to come over. Once I even paid them each a quarter to go out in the neighborhood and bring home some kids to play. They looked at me strangely, went out and brought kids in, played for a while, collected the quarters, and went back to playing with each other.

Ashley and Anna went Christmas shopping at Nordstrom when Ashley was in sixth grade and Anna was in ninth. They had their allowance money and some extra they had made doing household jobs. Ashley spotted a pair of sleek, black leather loafers that she knew I wanted, but the price was about ten dollars more than they had to spend. She approached the saleswoman, telling her that these would be the perfect shoes for their mom but that they were ten dollars short. She continued the negotiation until the saleswoman agreed to let them have the shoes at the price she wanted to pay.

Ashley played in the band at Hamilton Middle School. One day after school, she was waiting for the bus alone with her oboe in its case by her side. A tall, young man who had been hovering around outside the school walked over to where she was waiting, grabbed her oboe, and ran away with it. She found a large stick and ran after him, yelling, "Give me back my oboe. My grandpa gave it to me, and it is very expensive." She kept after him, waving her stick and yelling, until he dropped it and ran away.

First thing in the morning on weekends, still in her pajamas, teenage Ashley crossed the street to the house of our neighbor, Trisha, for waffles in her kitchen nook with stained glass windows of purple irises and stalks of bright-green leaves. Waffles led to making jewelry. Trisha and Ashley reveled in the colors, shapes, and origins of the beads, stringing together necklaces, bracelets, and earrings all day long. While working, they discussed and solved the world's problems. Since they believed they were so wise, they decided it would be a good idea to set up a table at Green Lake with a sign that said Free Advice—We Can Solve Your Problems. They had a lot of fun, and Trisha at age thirty-two said, "I felt like we were peers, like there wasn't any age difference." Those days, Ashley did not return home until around 4:00 p.m.

I liked to play tricks on Ashley and Anna. We had a big thing about See's Candies. Everybody in our family loved the candy and had jokes about it and lore about Mary See except for Ashley. We made Mary See into a national icon, pasting her head on our Valentine's Day cards, buying her cardboard playhouses, and filling them with stuffed bunnies and chickens. Mary See was like a family member you could not see. Ashley did not like the candy. This put a crimp in my holiday planning.

One day, I conspired with Anna to play a trick on Ashley with the See's Candies. I got some walkie-talkies from work, placed one behind the little trap door in Ashley's room, and gave Anna one to talk with. At bedtime, I went to Ashley's room with her, and Anna began speaking quaveringly into the walkie-talkie as the ghost of Mary See. "Ashley, this is Mary See. Why don't you like my candy?"

Ashley jumped out of bed and ran around the room, looking for where the voice was coming from. I denied hearing anything. She found the walkie-talkies against the trap door behind her bed, and Anna and I cracked up. I don't think Ashley ever thought it was funny.

AT FOURTEEN, ASHLEY WAS GETTING IN TROUBLE. NOT big trouble, just not adhering to my reasonable limits: being where she said she'd be or coming home on time, stuff like that. She tested limits often, and I had to set boundaries over and over. I knew I had to keep drawing lines, and I was getting weary of it.

Opening

One day during this phase, DJ, a friend from work, brought in two kittens she wanted to give away: a big, male calico and a little, gray, fluffy female tabby. Exasperated by Ashley's behavior and having to be the heavy day in and out, I thought I'd interrupt the cycle. I brought the tabby home, put her in a box, and took her to the park where Ashley was again crossing a behavioral line I had set. Instead of laying down the law, I said, "Go over to the box and open it." She walked over to it and crouched down on the grass. When she opened the lid, out popped the gray fluff ball. Surprised and delighted, she promptly named her Carmella after a friend she met at school. She loved the kitten through the years and came home to visit her after she graduated from high school and lived at home only in the summer.

There were still lines to draw, but our time at home did soften.

A Middle School Friend Shared:

Among the kids at school, I was that immigrant girl from a land far away. Born to Kurdish parents from Tehran, my family spoke Farsi at home, so I was slow to learn. My English was broken in sixth grade, and I was unable to speak English fluently and confidently until seventh or eighth grade. Still learning and absorbing the American culture of the eighties, I wanted to fit in badly but didn't know how.

Ashley was the prettiest, sassiest, and most popular girl in middle school. She always had a circle of girls around her at the lockers, outside of class, and in the cafeteria, doting on her as they laughed and giggled at things I didn't understand. They tried to look like her, copying her clothes and hair and all. I wondered what the fascination was all about.

One day after English class, Ashley walked up to me and pulled me by my arm into her circle of friends as if to say "this is where you belong." After that, I couldn't wait to get my hair permed just like hers and saved for months to buy a black leather jacket like hers.

Her kindness pulled me in. I remember she said to me one day when I was feeling vulnerable about being different, "You are not different. You are exotic." I didn't know what that word meant, but when I looked it up in my nerdy pocket dictionary, I remember feeling so good.

Purely coincidentally, when we ended up at the same high school many districts away, she was still an instant success, rising to the highest ranks of Shorewood's caste system, a cheerleader and all, but she never walked by me in the halls without stopping to say hello. Never did she not take note of me in the stands. We spent four years of high school like this.

Opening

The last time I saw Ashley was on a bridge at University of Washington. We were no more than twenty-two. She saw me and stopped instantly. Although she was in a hurry, we exchanged exciting words about graduating and our next chapter of life. Many years had passed from those years in middle school, but that same kindness that dominated her behavior during those formative years dominated her persona as a young lady.

—*Katayoun Rezaiamiri*

AFTER HIGH SCHOOL, ASHLEY CHOSE TO ATTEND UNIVERSITY of Washington. She joined a sorority, Kappa Kappa Gamma, and was active on and off campus. She worked as a nanny or in a deli. Her junior year, she travelled with a group of friends on an accredited trip to Ecuador, and a photo of her wearing a backpack half her size became one of my favorites. She double majored in communications and journalism.

During those years, I was busy, and she was busy. I remember she was surprised at how many of her friends were becoming part of a couple. She had dated but didn't see why her friends wanted to be so settled. She got bored. I thought, *She hasn't fallen in love yet.*

Firefly

A Friend from College Shared:

Ashley was my "little sister" in the sorority. She was so funny and dynamic, and everyone loved her and wanted to be around her. After she became my little sister the first quarter in college, we roomed together the next quarter. We were assigned the room "Mood" that overlooked the walkway leading up to the house. The previous October, she and I had needed costumes for a Halloween party. We couldn't find anything we liked, but we found these latex grandma masks that made us laugh and laugh. They covered our entire heads. Picture a movie-quality old lady face and a kerchief tied around the back. When they were on, you could not identify who was underneath. We wore them to a party and refused to take them off all night. Our greatest joy was to put the masks on, hang out the window of Mood, and shout at the guys coming to pick up people for dates in a quavering, old lady voice. It was hours of entertainment.

I had this horoscope calendar that year, and every day was terrible. We would laugh before I ripped it off and say, "Maybe today will be good." Nope. She would do this Oliver Twist imitation and sing the song from the musical in a Cockney accent, "Consider yourself at home," and it made me laugh so hard. We loved living in that room together, and

Opening

I could have lived with her for the rest of college! We were always great friends who got along, and that was how Ashley was with everyone. She was funny and cool, and everyone wanted to be around her all the time. I just loved her.
—*Alison Evans Shea*

College Portrait

Spreading Her Wings

When Ashley was a junior at the university, she came home for a visit one weekend. That morning, she came downstairs from her attic bedroom looking intensely agitated and asked me to please interpret a dream she had that night. This was an unusual request. Although I had only learned a little about interpreting dreams in the clinical psychology master's degree program at Antioch, I occasionally gave the amateur interpretation. It had been a few years since the last request. She washed her face, brushed her hair, and sat cross-legged on our pale-blue sectional couch to tell me her dream.

Looking tired, she explained that in the dream, she dug in dirt with her hands for what seemed like hours all night, digging and digging. She continued digging but was exhausted and stopped, intending to give up, thinking her body could no longer endure. She said, "I used all my strength and finally had enough life force to push my way down to red, green, and white stones." That culminated the dream. She continued to be shaken by it as though she had been digging all night. "What does this mean?"

I was disturbed that she was so shaken and told her, "I don't have an answer for you, but I will think about it and let you know when and if anything becomes clear."

I thought all day long and overnight about her dream, coming up with little. I told her, "That was an important dream, and we might not be able to figure it out until a later

Opening

time." I added, "Maybe the red, green, and white stones symbolize your Italian heritage. Wouldn't it be great to have a ring made out of those stones?" That was about as clear as I could get. I wasn't very helpful.

That was not the end of it. Her dream launched my two-year, on-and-off search for a ring that had red, green, and white stones in one setting. It became a treasure hunt. I thought that at some important time, I would give Ashley a ring with all the colored stones. I thought that she didn't need another ring, as she had several special rings already. In spite of this, I found myself looking for this imagined ring every time I passed a jewelry store in Seattle or Bellevue and on business trips. Nowhere did I find this particular combination of colors. I found it interesting after the search began that I was the one looking for the ring. I said to myself, *Jane, stop. Why are you so preoccupied with Ashley's dream? This is her dream, not yours. This is an odd thing to do*. Despite this thought, I continued looking.

ONE EVENING AFTER THANKSGIVING DURING HER SENIOR year at UW, Ashley called from an apartment she shared with some friends. "Mom, I want you to come to church with me on Christmas Eve, so you need to finish wrapping your presents before then." She was insistent.

On Christmas Eve, while many families are celebrating, opening gifts, attending church, or singing carols, I'm usually home wrapping presents until the Pope concludes Mass at St. Peter's Basilica at 2:30 a.m. Every year I vow to space out the wrapping during the weeks before Christmas. Even one or two packages before the deadline would get me to bed by midnight.

I was surprised by her request and promised to get the wrapping done ahead of time for once. That was the end of the conversation—a simple request to attend church with her. Not knowing she went to church in college, I was dumbfounded. When she and Anna were young, we went off and on to several different churches but were not regular attendees. She never mentioned going to church, not even once. I thought, *Well, if anything can get me to wrap early, this is it.*

As the deadline approached, I managed to wrap 30 percent of the packages before Christmas Eve. Ashley had chosen University Presbyterian Church adjacent to the UW campus and four blocks away from her sorority. It was a large church, and I'd never been there before. We walked through the doors and down the aisle and sat on the side section about a third of the way up. Lots of young families with excited kids were squirming around us. As the service began, more children came on stage, acting out the Christmas pageant: Mary, Joseph, shepherds, angels, animals, and kings.

Disappointed, Ashley said, "Oh no, this is not the kind of service I wanted you to see. I wanted you to see a regular adult service." She looked me in the eye and said out of the blue, "This is the place." Again with emphasis, "This is the place."

I didn't know what to say. What did she mean? We sat there in silence. She didn't explain further. She sounded serious and definite.

By Ashley's senior year at UW, she was focused on traveling the summer after graduation. The plan was to travel to Europe with girlfriends. As the year progressed, she worked to make money for the trip: making sandwiches in a deli, waitressing, and working as a nanny. Her girlfriends began dropping out of the travel plans for various reasons. Still determined to travel, Ashley kept working to make enough money to do so. Around that time, she met Tyler, a kindhearted, fun-loving, adventurous young man who lived in the fraternity across the street. They began dating in her senior year, became good friends, and fell in love.

Tyler also planned to travel after graduation. He was an experienced traveler, and his plans extended to more of an Asian experience. The European plans had fallen through, and Ashley decided to join Tyler on a trip to Asia. I didn't want her to go that far. She continued to work, waitressing at Brad's Swingside Café, a neighborhood Italian restaurant. Once I realized how set she was on the trip, I would have dinner there, and close to her last day, I left her a hundred dollar tip.

Meanwhile, my cousin Nancy Russell came to visit. Our mothers were sisters, we had always been close, and she was Ashley's godmother. Nancy worked with a nongovernmental organization in Nepal, and Ashley had written to her about visiting once the trip planning went to her part of the world. When Nancy was in Seattle that spring on her annual leave, Ashley came and talked to her. The UW graduation was on June 10, 1995, and Ashley and Tyler planned to leave on their trip on July 17. Their itinerary would put them in Nepal in August, arriving on August 22 by way of India. Nancy didn't get many visitors, so they were both excited to plan this together. I told Ashley that if she was going to travel, go for it without feeling like she had to keep in touch all the time.

I was planning my own adventure. I had loved living in my bungalow home in the Seattle Green Lake neighborhood with Ashley and Anna for twenty years. In the spring of 1995, I received a call from an old friend from Bainbridge Island, telling me about an opportunity to house-sit on the waterfront on Bainbridge Island for a family planning a nine-month trip. My friend knew from my visits over the years that I had always wanted to try living there to see if I'd like to move there permanently. House-sitting would be a way to do that and experience the daily commute to work by ferry.

To make the move, I had to organize, clear, and store a house worth of accumulated furniture and clothes, conduct a garage sale, and rent out my house to three young men attending UW who also promised to care for Carmella, Ashley's fluffy, gray-striped tabby. Trisha helped me get ready. She promised to check on "the boys" throughout my time away.

While organizing, I put some of Ashley's old dolls in a cardboard box, closing the top. She looked upset and said, "Don't close the top. They won't be able to breathe." Concerned at the intensity of her plea, I said, "Ashley, they are dolls. They can't breathe."

"Yes, they can," she said. She would have none of it. I didn't close the top until she left the house later.

Before Ashley left on July 17, I asked her to come and see the Bainbridge Island house. She was adamant about not going. "No, Tyler and I will come visit you after we come back from the trip." The move to Bainbridge Island was timed for September 2, 1995.

Ashley was also preparing for her trip. I noticed that she was giving a lot of her clothes away such as a lovely, bulky wool sweater she bought on her trip to Ecuador the prior year as well as other pieces of clothing she would need when she returned and the weather turned cold. At one point, she asked, "Mom, do you think it's strange that I'm giving so many of my clothes and things away?" I did think it was strange, but I didn't want to add to her stress or make her feel weird, so I said no. I wish now that I had told her the truth. After she left on the trip, one of her friends told me Ashley had given her watch to her.

Firefly

I was surprised that Ashley invited me to a send-off gathering at a friend's apartment near UW. She and Tyler were flying out that night, and lots of her buddies were gathered there to wish them goodbye. Anna called me on my cell phone because she was worried she wouldn't reach Ashley before she left. I overheard Ashley tell a friend, "I need to get my mother out of here." Shortly thereafter, she walked with me out through the front door. It hurt my feelings. We stood on the porch. She was uncharacteristically rigid and cool, not warm or hugging like usual. I remember nervously standing there with my eyes fixed on the black, pinprick-sized birthmark on her right ear lobe.

Although we aren't Jewish, I had adapted the bat mitzvah custom of giving each girl a family heirloom ring as a coming-of-age ritual to remind them of the kind of strong, loving women they are descended from and as encouragement to continue growing into the lovely young women they were becoming. I had given Ashley my grandmother's gold wedding band when she turned fourteen. It was difficult to part with that gold band, as I had worn it every day since my grandmother died, but it was the ring she wanted, so I gave it to her.

As we stood uncomfortably on the porch, she took off the ring and handed it to me. Shocked, I felt like a steel rod went through the center of my body. I looked at her and saw on her stomach what looked like a picture of her intestinal tract (brown) and thought how strange it was that I would see that image.

That was the last time I saw her before her trip.

Opening

Morning Lane

It was bright and sunny on moving day, September 2, with the Cascade mountain range in striking, magnificent view as my girlfriends and I ferried to Bainbridge Island. We sat on the deck, drinking orange juice and strong coffee, eating fresh-baked scones, and enjoying the beauty of the day. I was filled with anticipation as we drove off the ferry and made the turns to the house: right on Day Road, left on Sunrise Drive, and right on Morning Lane. I loved that everything oriented toward morning and hoped living there would help me become a morning person.

Upon arriving, my friends and I flung open all the glass doors and windows, turned on the stereo and a *Mary Poppins* soundtrack at full volume, explored, and then relaxed in this idyllic setting. The house was in a casual Northwest style, situated directly on the waterfront with sweeping views of the Cascades. I climbed upstairs to the master bedroom that also had an expansive view of the water and mountains to spend a few moments to take in the glory and wonder. When I reached the bedroom window, tears came: a mix of gratitude for nature at my doorstep with a certain melancholy beneath. I looked out the window, taking in the glistening sun on the lapping shore, thanking God for the enormity of this gift and saying to myself, *I hope this is not a consolation prize.*

Are you flying through the night
Looking where to find me?
Nay, I travel with a light
For the folks behind me.

—John B. Tabb, "The Fire-Fly"[4]

PART II
The Search

The phone rang, and it was Nancy. "I don't want you to panic, but Ashley and Tyler did not arrive when I went to pick them up at the airport."

I knew that Ashley and Tyler planned to visit Nancy in Nepal, but I didn't know the date. She said she had gone to the airport for the flight from India on the date they had been expected to arrive. Delays from India were not uncommon, so she met the flight again the next two days. "I don't want you to panic," she repeated. She was going to go to the airport again.

When I hung up, I felt nauseated and scared. I laid down on the couch and fell fast asleep. With all of my being, I hoped and prayed that everything would be fine.

Firefly

Nancy Russell

In 1993, I was hired to direct a community-based family planning project in Nepal for an organization called Center for Development and Population Activities (CEDPA) based in Washington, DC and funded by United States Aid for International Development (USAID). When I had been at my job for about two years, I received a graduation announcement from Ashley. At that time, I had no email and relied on getting mail through my home office in Washington, DC. It was always exciting to get letters or cards, but this card was special. Ashley added a note telling me that she and her boyfriend were going to travel around the world after graduation, and she wanted to stop by and visit me.

I was excited by this prospect. She was one of few people in my family who wanted to visit me, and she was the only one of the younger cousins or nieces and nephews who seemed to love the idea of travel and life in other cultures like I did. I felt a special bond with her. She was always a child filled with spark and curiosity. "And her face is very serious until she smiles, and then the sun lights up the world." To me, that quote from Children of Happiness *by Anne Cameron was Ashley.*

Jane asked my husband and me to be her daughters' godparents. We had had many pregnancies and a failed adoption.

Jane wanted to give me a special role with her children, and I was honored. I took it seriously but mostly remembered birthdays and visited when possible.

I always assumed that my role would be to provide them love and care if something happened to Jane. It never occurred to me that something would happen to Anna or Ashley. When Ashley was missing, I told people she was my niece. To say that I was her godmother made me feel that I was neglecting my role and could not protect her as I should. It was too heavy a term, but "cousin" was too removed. I loved Jane like a sister, so "niece" did not seem too much of a stretch.

I loved Jane and the girls and was thrilled that Ashley put me on her itinerary. I looked forward to sharing my life in Nepal with her.

As I remember, I received the note in May or June. Soon after, I went to Portland and Seattle for my home leave. I visited Jane, and Ashley came over to see me. We talked about Nepal, and I cautioned her that August was a bad time to trek due to the monsoon rains. I assured her that I would arrange something for her to do while they were in Nepal. When we parted, I knew that Ashley and Tyler would arrive in Nepal on August 22. I returned to Nepal, excited to plan for their visit and pleased to see how much Ashley looked forward to her trip and to visiting me in Nepal.

During the next month, I went on a short trek outside of Kathmandu and talked to guides about safe places to trek in

Firefly

August. One Saturday in late July or August, I returned to my flat from shopping and learned from my cook, Hasta, that Ashley had called from India to say they had had a change in plans and would arrive September 8 instead of August 22. I was so disappointed that I quizzed Hasta about the call. He spoke English well, but it was possible he had misunderstood the message over the phone depending on the connection. I hoped she would call again, but she did not.

On September 8, I had Hasta bake an apple pie, and it was in process when I left for the airport. I waited for arrivals in the upstairs restaurant with a full view of the planes that landed. I got there early because I was full of anticipation and excitement. The plane landed on time on a clear fall day, and I watched anxiously as the passengers disembarked at the front and back of the plane and watched carefully to be sure I spotted Ashley. There were lots of young people with backpacks coming from India. I watched until the last person and crew disembarked.

As soon as I was aware they weren't there, I stood up in disbelief and walked quickly down a hallway that must have been marked as the area where the computers were that recorded all the passengers. I don't remember how I found the office, but I was so worried about Ashley and Tyler that I left my purse where I had been sitting, and my wallet and camera were stolen. We did not have cell phones then, so I could not call a friend. I asked to see the passenger list for the flight. As I remember, their names were on the list, but they were not on the plane.

The Search

I had a car and driver and had rented a special car larger than the usual remodeled taxi so that it would be big enough for their luggage. I got in the car and did not talk to my driver. I could not explain to him what had happened in broken Nepali and English. I stared straight ahead as we took the route back to my house, almost in a trance. When I got home, Hasta had gone home, and the apple pie was cooling on the kitchen counter.

I called friends and met up with them to get their advice and support, as I was shaken and felt disoriented. Everyone was sure Ashley and Tyler had gotten delayed. I found that their tickets were issued in Goa, a popular beach resort, and my friends were sure they had decided to hang out a few more days on the beach. I knew that was not the case. Ashley had planned this trip carefully.

For the next two or three days, maybe longer, I went to the airport every day and checked the computer passenger lists. It became clear that they were not coming. I put off calling Jane as long as I could, as I did not want to alarm her. After one more airport visit, I asked her to fax me a photo of Ashley. I remember watching in disbelief as it came through the fax machine. It was her graduation photo, and she looked so beautiful. I made the photo into a flyer that gave her name and the details about their expected arrival. The headline was MISSING. I had never expected to be posting flyers like these. My office staff and friends helped me to post them. I reached out to the Red Cross—my hope was that someone traveling from India would have met them.

Presence

After taking in the full, sweeping, water-up-to-the windows view, one of the first things I did after arriving for my nine-month stay at the Bainbridge Island house was to plop onto the blue-and-white-striped loveseat and page through the coffee table book in front of me. Windows all around me, in the center of the couch, I felt like a sailor in a boat as I read a page juxtaposed by a photo of Agate Pass Bridge and blue water beneath a caption by Chief Seattle. The chief's words introduced me and framed my time in this beautiful place. Some months later, I discovered that Chief Seattle, for whom the city is named, was buried in the tiny town of Suquamish, named after his tribe, only minutes north from the house.

> Our dead never forget this beautiful world that gave them being. They still love its verdant valleys, its murmuring rivers, its magnificent mountains, sequestered vales and verdant lined lakes and bays, and ever yearn in tender fond affection over the lonely hearted living, and often return from the happy hunting ground to visit, guide, console, and comfort them.
>
> And when the last red man shall have perished from the earth and his memory among white men shall have become a myth, these shores shall swarm with the invisible dead of my tribe, and when your children's children shall think themselves alone in the

field, the store, the shop, upon the highway or in the silence of the woods, they will not be alone.

—Chief Seattle, Chief of the Suquamish[5]

One should…be able to see things as hopeless and yet be determined to make them otherwise.

—F. Scott Fitzgerald[6]

An imposing, shiny, black digital clock radio, with one-inch-high numbers, stood on the counter between two sinks in the big, white-tiled bathroom at the Bainbridge Island house. The alarm worked fine, and I used it to help get me to work to catch the 7:10 a.m. ferry to Seattle at the beginning of my stay.

About the time I received the dreaded phone call from Nancy telling me Ashley and Tyler did not appear for her pickup in Kathmandu, the clock went dead. I figured it was broken, because there was nothing I could do to activate it again.

The broken radio marked the beginning of daily phone calls to Nancy, alerting the Red Cross search and rescue teams in Kathmandu and Delhi that put up photographs of Ashley with a description of Tyler all over the region. Nancy worked in this manner with the Red Cross for a week, and when there was no sign of Ashley or Tyler, it became more official with the families. Opening the search up to Ralph and Marlys was rough. I did not want to cede what little control I had. Tyler's parents were on their own around-the-world sailing trip, and we did not want to alarm them without cause that Ashley and Tyler were missing.

I BROUGHT TO THE BAINBRIDGE ISLAND HOUSE SEVERAL framed photographs of Anna and Ashley and a few of friends so I'd feel more at home. I put them atop a cabinet by the fireplace in the family room and a few by the windows by the back door. One day during the two-week period when we comprehended the seriousness of the situation, I walked down the stairs from the bedroom to the family room before I raced off to make the 7:10 morning ferry. Something was different in the room. I couldn't figure it out at first, but then I noticed that many of the pictures were turned over on their sides. There were no animals in the house to have upset the pictures. The following day, there was a high-pitched yet barely audible alarm, making it difficult to remain in the room for more than five minutes. I traced the noise to the machine that controlled the septic tank. The mechanic I called said there was nothing wrong with the machine, and there was no reason for the alarm.

I knew I couldn't go back and forth from holding onto hope and being fearful without descending into despair. I also knew that experiencing hope and fear simultaneously would make me crazy and render me unable to work or connect with people. I decided they were alive until there was absolute proof that they were dead. To do this, I had to connect moment to moment with the presence of God, visualizing an old-fashioned rope tow on a ski slope, letting the force of its power pull me up the mountain. If I didn't hang on tight with all my might, I would fall off. When I did fall off, as occasionally happened, I had to find my way back to the rope and grab on again.

Keeping myself distracted from the ever-present reality of Ashley's missing-ness through regular work was therapy. One woman in my department periodically came into my office and cleared out the mounds of paper that accumulated because of my lessened ability to make decisions. When home, I took to my bed, barely able to lift my leaden body upright. It was clear that if I kept up this behavior, I would soon be out of a job in addition to searching for my missing daughter.

I prayed continually. Although I'm not Catholic, I focused on Mary, identifying with her anguish over the death of her son. She helped me, but I needed someone more concrete, someone real. I tried hard to think of a role model who I could fully access who had endured anguish, pain, and uncertainty for a long time yet sustained hope, courage, and determination. I thought and thought. This was a difficult and specific job description to fill, and the image of my mother surfaced. I had called on her during difficult times in the past, and I could easily get a clear image of her even though she died over thirty years ago.

My mother had cancer from the time I was three years old until she died when I was seventeen. Besides the physical pain, Mom spent years not knowing whether the cancer had spread to other parts of her body. Treatment involved numerous operations. According to my grandmother, Mom had willed herself to stay alive until I graduated high school and my brother John began high school, which she did. For her strength of will, endurance, and sense of humor throughout the pain and waiting for answers, I chose her to focus on to endure the waiting, hoping, and fear during the search for Ashley.

Another thought emerged. A few years after Mom's death I read a children's book, *Remember the Secret* by Elisabeth Kübler-Ross. It claimed that if you needed a person who had died and asked them to come help you, they would be there for you. I had admired the work of Kübler-Ross for years and believed in her findings and research. In determining Mom was the person exemplifying the qualities I needed to sustain during the search, Kübler-Ross's book surfaced to the front of my mind. I prayed, *Mom, no matter where you are, whatever you are doing, I need you to get off work and come to be with me every minute. I need you to help me to keep going. I don't know how long it's going to take to find Ashley. I need you for the long haul, and I can't afford to lose my job. Of anyone I know, you had the courage not to give up but commit to living while enduring years of suffering, waiting for answers.*

After I made the request for her help, throughout the search of four months, I managed to get up and go to work from September through January. It was as though my mother jumped inside me, giving me the energy I didn't have.

I rode the ferry to my downtown Seattle office and returned by ferry to the Bainbridge Island house. Sometimes I was too tired to take the ferry home and stayed in Seattle with friends. Doris, my stepmom, was concerned, saying, "I don't think you should be staying alone, isolated in the big house."

I did not feel alone, but I would have felt the way Doris did about someone else in my situation. My friend Carol Angel (her real name) stayed with me some days in the week, yet when I stayed in town with friends, I soon felt restless to be at home.

When I walked in the door after one of the Seattle stays, deep peace and warmth welcomed me. It was as if there was a family room of visitors I could not see, taking up space. Before her trip, Ashley told me, when she wouldn't come with me to check out the Bainbridge Island house, that she and Tyler would come back and stay with me when the trip was over. I only knew that I could not be away from the house for more than two days before needing to experience the peace and love I felt there.

"Doris, I don't think I'm alone."

Nancy

Many of my American and European friends in Nepal were practicing Buddhists. Nepal is a spiritual place. Buddha was born in Nepal, and pilgrimages to his birthplace are common. Trekking to temples high in the mountains can be a spiritual experience. Over the weeks and then months that Ashley's whereabouts were unknown, I lit candles at Buddhist temples and visited some.

A good friend, Paul, took me to meet some Buddhist monks he knew in Katmandu who often read horoscopes and were known to have special talents at reading the future. He translated for me as I asked them if they knew where Ashley was. I heard the chants and smelled the incense. It felt like I was going to an oracle. The room was full of colorful, old, silk thangka paintings and white silk scarves. Four or five old men sat with their legs crossed on low benches with big wooden books in front of them. They wore dark-red robes and looked kind and peaceful. They listened as Paul translated, were quiet, and then conferred. They thought she and Tyler were well and in the Himalayas. Paul hugged me, and I went down the narrow, worn stone stairs with new confidence, although later we realized that they had not said they were alive. "Well" could also mean at peace. In their world, life on earth wasn't the only way to be well. We didn't know, and I again lost my confidence that they were alive.

Another good friend, Lynn, took me to Boudha, a holy stupa surrounded by temples. We went to a lecture by Guru Rinpoche. Dozens of people, mostly European dharma students, were in the room, sitting on the floor with their legs crossed. He spoke about appreciating life and being kind and calm. The Tibetan monks were often funny, so laughter was followed by attentive silence. Afterwards, Lynn took me to speak with him. I told him about Ashley, and he too assured me she was alive, but I was not convinced and went home without much consolation.

All the Buddhist monks were Nepali or Tibetan. They wore red robes and yellow silk underneath. They were calm and felt connected to something otherworldly. The temples were painted in red, yellow, green, blue, and white, the colors of prayer flags. The colors represented the elements of the universe including the earth and sky. I felt calmed in the presence of the people, but nothing quelled my anxiety.

The longer we did not find evidence of Ashley and Tyler being alive, it was hard to hold out hope. Jane had strong faith and believed they were, and I supported her in that *belief with as much confidence as I could find in myself. I called at Thanksgiving when Jane was with her family. I remember a tearful conversation with Jane's stepmother, Doris, who was worried. I was glad Jane had her family and I had my friends. Those months were desperate.*

Crossings

When the early stage of the Red Cross search yielded nothing, I learned of a psychic from a reliable source who thought she might be able to help locate Ashley and Tyler. A lovely, kind woman, Joyce welcomed me into her office and explained how she worked in situations like ours where people were missing. "I use a map of the area and hold a pendulum over the map. The pendulum will start to swing in the direction of the location of the missing people."

She held the pendulum over the map of India for several minutes, but it did not move. That scared me. She suggested that Ashley and Tyler might be in a particular region of India (I no longer remember which one).

Tyler's parents had joined forces with our family to create a search committee. In November, Ralph and Tyler's father scheduled a flight to India to search personally. Tyler's parents and I had often gathered at Ralph and Marlys's home during the search. Part of the reason for gathering there was that Tyler's parents had already begun their sailing trip around the world shortly before they found out that Ashley and Tyler were missing. They were unable to return to their home because it was rented to caretakers. With my need to ferry back and forth from Seattle to Bainbridge Island, I stayed overnight with Ralph and Marlys on several occasions.

RALPH AND TYLER'S DAD HAD JUST RETURNED FROM A disappointing search in northern India. They found next to nothing that would give any of us hope of finding Ashley and Tyler, even though they had managed to find a backpacker's hotel where they had stayed in Manali and a bank where Tyler had cashed a traveler's check. There was no further trace of Ashley and Tyler. Even though Secretary of State Warren Christopher and Congressman Norm Dicks graciously provided diplomatic contacts at the US Embassy and the India Ministry of Home Affairs in New Delhi, the fathers returned to Seattle a few weeks later right before Thanksgiving with little good news to report.

AT THANKSGIVING, THE WHOLE FAMILY GATHERED AT THE Bainbridge Island house for dinner except for Anna who was sequestered in Colorado with her boyfriend Steve teaching preschoolers how to ski.

Pathos described the mood. In despair after having returned from India, Ralph feared the worst. No one would come right out and say it—the elephant in the room was that Ashley was dead. Holding onto that rope tow with a fierce grip for the sake of sanity, I steadfastly maintained that Ashley and Tyler were alive. Anna was of the same opinion, but she was in Colorado. Suffice it to say I felt alone in my view and disturbed mightily.

John said the next day, "That was the worst Thanksgiving we've ever had."

After everyone went home about 7:00 p.m., I fell asleep and woke up to an unusually sunny day for a Seattle November. Shaken by the sadness of the evening before, I placed myself directly in the path of the brilliant sun, soaked it in, and began singing the song I used to sing to my kids before bedtime: "You are my sunshine, my only sunshine, you make me happy when skies are gray. You'll never know, dear, how much I love you. Please don't take my sunshine away."[7] I let in what the others had said the night before for a moment and then clamped it back, replacing it with the remaining hope that she lived.

I ran upstairs to the bathroom where I found the digital clock radio had come alive with its brightly lit numbers and the sound of music.

The onslaught of winter weather in the Himalayas was not far away, so a critical decision had to be made. We needed professional help. We hired Kroll Associates, an investigative agency, to organize an international search with help from donations. One of the principals at Kroll, Arish Turle, was a former Scotland Yard detective who acted as point person. Based in the United Kingdom, Kroll had many contacts in India, given its former state as a colony.

"How soon can you get here?"

"How long can you stay?"

During these months, many angels appeared in my life including friends like Carol Angel. She is a slight, kind woman with soft, platinum hair. Everything about her is angelic except her subtle, dry sense of humor. I don't imagine angels with senses of humor, but maybe they have them. Formerly an attorney and editor for *Washington Journal*, a legal publication, she was often writing articles for the paper or a children's book in her spare time.

Carol saved my life day by day. When we declared that something was wrong and decided to launch a search, I called her and asked her to come stay with me. She said, "When do you want me?" I said, "As soon as you can get here, for as long as you can stay." She said, "Okay. I can be there tomorrow."

That was the beginning of a long ride with a dear friend who was a quiet, gentle, loving, humorous presence. We ate Dutch Babies sprinkled with powdered sugar, lemon juice squeezed on top, nearly every morning when she came for breakfast. She obliged my need to make weekly trips to nearby Poulsbo, affectionately known as "Little Norway." We stopped at Sluys Poulsbo Bakery for a maple bar man (a maple bar shaped like a gingerbread man, only way bigger) and visited the quilt store to ask questions of an expert seamstress named Norma. We hung out in the pharmacy where they sold old-time illustrated greeting cards with chickens pulling wagons, bunnies at the circus, and girls with pinwheel dresses. After perusing the cards, we'd sit at the counter on bar stools for a mocha milkshake in a tall Viking glass.

In December, family members planned to celebrate Christmas in Colorado where Anna and Steve lived, and Ralph and Marlys had a winter home. I told Carol, "I'm not going to put up a Christmas tree. I won't be around, and I am way too tired to deal with it."

One Friday night near Christmas, I got home after book club to see Carol typing on her laptop at the kitchen counter, flanked by the smallest live Christmas tree I had ever seen, decorated with gold fuzzy swags and ornaments. A brown teddy bear in a sleigh-shaped basket adorned with a velvet, wine-colored bow rested next to the tree.

The Search

THE IN-BETWEEN WITH ANNA

I needed to be with Anna not only because Christmas without her would not be a true Christmas but also because, despite mounting evidence to the contrary, she and I continued to hold out hope that Ashley and Tyler would come back. I began planning a trip to Colorado.

Although tempted to buy a present for Ashley, when I asked Janet for her opinion, I was surprised at her emphatic "No!" I decided to at least look for special Christmas ornaments for both Ashley and Anna, as I had traditionally done since the girls were teenagers. In prior years, I sought out old-fashioned glass ornaments representing experiences they were having that particular year. I found a colorful skier ornament for Anna and a globe of the earth with deep blue for water and green for continents. *It's perfect. She's somewhere on the earth. We just don't know where yet.*

I carefully wrapped the fragile ornaments with several layers of paper for the trip. After arriving at Anna and Steve's apartment, I unwrapped and hung the brightly colored skier. While unfolding the layers of paper surrounding the globe, a piece fell out into my hand, revealing a half-inch hole in the glass. I did not hang the broken globe but did not throw it away. I didn't know what to do with it. The hole in the middle scared me, as I again confronted the possibility that Ashley had blasted her way out of the planet.

That night, Anna and I went to an ice-skating show. We had good seats a few rows back from the ice. Skaters in colorful costumes came on and off the ice while music played in the background. I was grateful for the time alone with Anna after being in separate locations throughout the search.

We watched the skaters with delight, and a tall man and a woman wearing a short, sparkly, aqua-blue skirt danced out on the ice. As they skated, the music changed to "Somewhere Out There" from *An American Tail*.[8] The movie is about Fievel Mousekewitz, a mouse who is separated from his parents when he is thrown from a ship's deck during a wild storm. He scours the new and strange New York City to find his family. Unfortunately, it seems to Fievel's family that their son is dead and lost at sea, and they sadly go on with their lives without him. Only Tanya, Fievel's older sister, believes that he is alive.

> "That we'll find one another in that big
> somewhere out there"[9]

Side by side, Anna and I looked at each other, listening and absorbing the words through the music and not ready to give up that Ashley was somewhere out there.

> O Mouse, do you know the way out of this pool? I am very tired of swimming about here, O Mouse!
> —Lewis Carroll, *Alice's Adventures in Wonderland* [10]

After Christmas, I felt physically worn down. My no-holds-barred strategy of holding out hope unless Ashley and Tyler were pronounced dead was fraying. Unraveling in this cloudy state of mind and body on a weekday morning, I stayed home from work. I was barely awake, in my pajamas, when the phone rang. It was Joyce, the psychic I had visited nearly four months earlier. She said, "I am getting messages interrupting me on my computer that you need encouragement and support. They are insistent, so that's why I am calling."

Surprised listening to her, I felt uplifted and strengthened. I managed to fight off the encroaching flu for a few more days.

END OF THE SEARCH

On January 10 at 8:30 a.m., the families were scheduled to meet at Ralph's law firm to get the report from Arish Turle. I thought I should spend the night before in Seattle because I was so tired and might not have enough energy, would screw something up, and would miss the meeting. I should have paid attention to my inner warning but instead accused myself of being a wimp. I could get up and get to the meeting.

I woke as usual at 6:15 and drove to the ferry, walked up the gangway, and found a seat upstairs at a long, beige Formica table with a window looking out on utter winter blackness. It was not yet dawn, and I decided to make use of the twenty-five-minute commute to edit a request for proposal for our land use lawyer at work. *I'm going to focus on this project and not think about the meeting.* I focused too intently as the man and woman next to me left the table. The entire cafeteria of people filed out from their seats like Catholics at Mass. I thought, *I've still got time. I'll finish this section and then leave. People get in a snit about racing off the boat.*

When I looked up, there was no one else around me, and it was still dark outside the windows. I packed up my papers and shoved them into my briefcase for the uphill trek to the office. I walked to the gangplank to see whitecaps generated by the boat's engine with the chain over the off-ramp, about twelve feet separating the boat from the slip. The ferry was on its way back to Bainbridge Island, and I was headed away from Seattle. I had to ride back to Bainbridge Island, run off the boat to call Ralph and tell him that I didn't get off the boat, and ride the ferry to Seattle again. I hated calling to tell him this, but he was pretty good about the whole thing. He laughed. I said, "Please start the meeting without me. I'll get there as soon as I can."

While crossing back again, I sat on the vinyl bench across from two lawyer friends, Vern and Jeff. The sun beaming in on us outlined the Cascades through the adjacent window. I told them that I had missed an important meeting by not getting off the boat. Vern, the kind, soon-to-be retired gentleman, said, "Well, that must be a meeting you didn't want to attend."

I arrived at Ralph's office a half-hour into the phone meeting with Arish Turle. Tyler's parents, Ralph, and his law partner, Otto, were gathered around a long, oval conference table, crying. Arish had told the group that his Indian detectives had talked to shepherds in the mountains who saw a European couple swept away while trying to cross the Chandra River during a flash flood. Based on the shepherds' account, the conclusion was that Ashley and Tyler had drowned. The date matched when they would have been in a hurry to catch a plane to Kathmandu for the trek Nancy had arranged for them. The shepherds had a network among themselves but no formal reporting system to the government regarding the incident.

Ralph gently delivered the news to me that everyone else had heard from Arish. I was out of sync, and it didn't register. I told Otto, "I need to go back to work and finish a request for proposal due today."

He looked at me and said, "Jane, you won't be working today."

"I won't?"

"No, you will not be working today."

Marlys came in, and the three of us called Anna in Colorado. Devastated from all this, everybody left with their respective spouses, and I stayed with Ralph's secretary, a kind, beautiful woman who asked me, "Would you like me to call your office?" I thought that was a good idea, because I wasn't sure how I was going to get the information out and get back to the office to wind up the RFP and keep going. Much relieved, I said yes and waited for her to make the calls.

I called Ellen. She and I had become good friends, and our offices were next to one another at the firm. On the days I was too tired to commute to Bainbridge Island, she invited me to stay at her house in Seattle. She knew I had the meeting in Ralph's office. I said, "Ellen, Ashley drowned. I have to get to the office. I'm walking back and should get there in twenty minutes. Please be in my office."

The walk back to the office was long and strange. My new wide, flowing, black, ankle-length raincoat blew around me like Darth Vader. That's what I remember most—trudging back in the cold in the black coat. I knew I needed to hand off the proposal and get out of there quickly. Pushing the elevator button in the City Centre Building, Chihuly art glass sprinkled all around and buoyed by gray-and-white marble, I rose through the column, surfacing at the law firm. As the elevator doors opened, Ellen stood in front of me. Surprised by her instantaneous appearance, I walked alongside her to my office, raincoat still flowing. On the way, we passed

Stephanie, who sat across from my office, visible from the window, sobbing. As assistant to the chief operating officer, no doubt Stephanie had been the first to receive the phone call and information about Ashley that was traveling ahead of me.

Ellen and I entered my office and closed the door, aware of Stephanie outside. The telephone rang. It was Ralph. "Would you like to hear what happened from Arish Turle directly?"

Grateful for this kindness, I said, "I would like that. Thank you."

A few minutes later, Arish called, and I asked Ellen to stay with me to hear what he said.

He ran through the scenario that he had told the people in the meeting. He said, "It cannot be absolutely proven that Ashley and Tyler drowned, but the shepherds said they saw two Europeans attempting to cross the river, then fall, and be carried away by the raging current. None of them could help without endangering their own lives."

Knowing Arish had a daughter, I asked, "If your daughter was missing and you heard this scenario through your detectives from the shepherds, would you conclude that they drowned?"

"Yes," he said.

Having met the serious former Scotland Yard man in person, I accepted this finality. All the while, Ellen sat quietly next to me. In the middle of Arish's discourse, Chuck E., an old friend and partner in the firm, came into my office and stood behind us. It was good to have these dear friends close.

Firefly

Four months after the day they did not arrive in Kathmandu, the search ended. Ashley and Tyler had been swept away and drowned on September 4, 1995.

I DON'T KNOW HOW I MANAGED TO LEAVE THE OFFICE BY myself, but I walked down the hill from Fourth Avenue to the Bainbridge Island ferry and made it to the house on Morning Lane. I opened the door, walked upstairs, and laid on the bed with my arms out stretched, palms up, as Chief Dan George did playing Grandfather in the 1970 movie, *Little Big Man*, trying out his method of dying with dignity after his entire village was slaughtered because it was "a good day to die."

Asking to be taken up, hoping that I would be, laying on the bed for thirty minutes and still wide awake, I opened my eyes, got up, and said like Grandfather, "I guess it's not today." Angry as hell, I declared, "God, if you're not going to take me up, I am going to live the best goddamn life I can. I'm not going to let this take me down." A few minutes later: "I have one request. I want to see beneath the veil. At least grant me that, at least a glimpse."

Much later when I watched *Little Big Man* again, I realized I'd forgotten the grandfather character also says, "Sometimes the magic works, and sometimes it doesn't."

The Search

From that day of learning the truth, even though there were times when it seemed too hard, I came back to having made a choice. "This isn't going to take me down. I'm going to live the best goddamn life I can. Help me see beneath the veil."

Of Light

    Sometimes you move
    toward the light.
    Sometimes the light
    moves toward you.

—J. A.

PART III

Beyond

Nancy

On January 11, 1996, I was getting ready to go on a field trip to a remote part of Nepal. I had not left Kathmandu often since September, as I was always waiting for a call from Jane. I knew that there was a search going on, but I had to go on this field trip to monitor the activities and office of the regions where our program worked. About 5:00 a.m., as I was about to leave, the phone rang. It was Jane. She had just learned that Ashley and Tyler had drowned on September 4. They had already died by the time I went to meet them at the airport. I assured Jane that I would get on a plane that day. With lots of help, I managed to get a flight that night.

Firefly

Ralph and Marlys took the lead on the memorial. Anna and Steve came home from Colorado. Andrew, Ashley and Anna's brother, came home from Pullman, Washington, where he was attending Washington State University. I was able to get on the rolls at Saint Mark's Episcopal Cathedral where I'd been attending services so that the memorial could be held at that amazing place on Wednesday, January 17, 1996, a week after the official news was received. Ralph, along with Tyler's family, focused on the content, and Marlys coordinated the music with members of the Seattle Symphony. I managed to have a favorite photo of Ashley from her time in Ecuador printed poster-size to be set up at the memorial. Little did I know how important this big picture would become in my life.

A local reporter had been following the search, and I was told there would be a story in the paper. As I waited at Sea-Tac Airport for Nancy to arrive from Nepal, I picked up the *Seattle Post-Intelligencer* and was shocked to see that Ashley and Tyler's photos and story were on the front page: *Lives of Man, Woman Who Died In India Shone Brightly, Briefly—Investigation Finds Two UW Graduates Were Swept to Deaths in Flooding River*. I lost it, sobbing in the little concession stand.

Ellen became a shepherd and took the role to another level. She drove me to Trisha's house and to the airport to meet Nancy's flight from Nepal. She made a schedule of people to be with me night and day for several weeks before and after the memorial, and she made sure someone was with me around the clock.

I watched as people came in, brought food, slept, and hung out. People took turns sleeping with me each night. I would turn over, and there would be a different person next to me. The night before the memorial, I turned over, and there was Ellen. I thought, *She should not have this hard duty. Even though we have become close friends, working together at the law firm, she is my newest friend.*

I woke up that Wednesday morning, the sun streaming in. I thought this would be a good morning to walk the beach, but I couldn't get up. I asked if people would let me sleep and sleep and sleep. It was getting late, and Nancy came into the bedroom. "Jane, you need to get up now, or you will miss the memorial."

I got dressed and headed to the ferry for the trip to Saint Mark's Episcopal Cathedral. At the memorial, with Anna sitting next to me, I listened as Ralph and Tyler's dad offered eulogies on behalf of our families. Nancy shared the poem "Children of Happiness" from *Daughters of Copper Woman*. Members of the Seattle Symphony played Barber's "Adagio for Strings" and "The Trumpet Shall Sound" from Handel's *Messiah*. There was a gathering for friends and family after the memorial at Ralph and Marlys's home.

Firefly

On the night after the memorial, J. E., an old friend who lived on Bainbridge Island, took two fat, white, twenty-four-inch-tall column candles, placed them in glass covers, and burned them all night in her house. When I arrived home from the service, she came rolling along in her bright-red Volvo station wagon, crunching down the gravel driveway. After jumping out of her car, she gingerly carried each lit candle, one at a time, and carefully placed them on the porch. Oh so carefully she guarded each candle with her body so the light would keep burning. To no avail—both candles went out promptly when she reached the porch. She became shaken and visibly upset. I reassured her that it was okay. The candles were home.

Beyond

Ashley in Ecuador
Memorial Photograph

Firefly

Signs

A week or so after moving to Bainbridge Island, I took a walk on the beach with friends, picking up round stones as we went along. I gathered a coatload of them and, when I returned home, sorted through them until I found the two smoothest oval gray ones. I wasn't thinking of Ashley, but I remember saying, "You only need two."

Letting all the others drop from my coat to the sand, I walked inside the house and placed the favored stones on the kitchen counter. Then I moved them to the table. I kept moving them around, finding myself staring at them during conversations with friends who came to visit during the day. Later that night, I brought them upstairs to my bedroom and set them on the bedside table where I could keep my eye on them. Not satisfied, I took them to bed with me and held one in each hand. After a few days of sleeping with the rocks, I said to myself, *Jane, you are nuts. You are sleeping with rocks.* I made myself put them on the shelf in my bedroom.

Four months later, after the memorial, in a rare moment when I was alone, looking out at the water from my bedroom window, I asked the question that had bothered me since I learned Ashley had died. I felt as her mother that I would have known that she died, but I had not. I asked her, *Ashley, since we are mother and daughter and so close, how did I not know that you died? How come you didn't tell me somehow?*

I had an immediate vision of the stones: finding them, sorting them, watching them, being inextricably drawn to them, moving them around the house with me, and sleeping with them. I was grateful.

> The little ones you can / hold in your hands, their heartbeats / so secret, so hidden it may take years / before, finally you hear them.
> —Mary Oliver, *Swan: Poems and Prose Poems*[11]

AFTER THE MEMORIAL, I WOKE UP EVERY MORNING WANTing a maple bar man. I couldn't get enough of them and drove to Poulsbo most mornings. I loved the maple-y taste. I would bite off the head first, then the arms, and then the legs. Nothing else seemed to satisfy me like maple bar man.

A few days after the memorial, my friend, Woody, insisted that I leave the house and join her for dinner. She lived with her husband, Bernie, in a quaint cottage overlooking Puget Sound. Her mother was Native American of the Spokane tribe. Her father had died that summer before we knew Ashley was missing, and she had been grieving for him.

Sitting at Woody's dining room table, facing the fireplace, I spotted a large, black crow decoy on the mantle. I asked her about it, and she said she saw the crow in a shop in Poulsbo and bought it a few days after her dad died. Throughout the dinner, I could not keep my eyes off that crow and asked her if there were any more in the store. She said she thought there were and told me how to find it.

I have never been an obsessive person. In fact, people consider me laid back. However, the obsessions began with an attraction to stones as if they were crying out to me, asking to be taken up and held day after day, night after night. Like the stones, I couldn't take my eyes off Woody's crow.

The next morning, I found the store in a house on a little hill in Poulsbo and bought two crows: one for me and one for Trisha. I sat on a wooden bench outside the store, calm and satisfied, looking at the crows on my left side with a maple bar man in my right hand.

> There was a time when ravens and crows were held sacred by almost all native peoples of the Americas. Ravens and crows were almost always considered to be messengers between the living and the spirit worlds...It was well known that Crow and Raven were medicine birds who could cross over to the Land of the Dead to bring back messages from departed loved ones.
> —Catherine Feher-Elston, *Ravensong: A Natural and Fabulous History of Ravens and Crows*[12]

Beyond

I returned to work three weeks after the memorial. Weather in January was typically gray with light rain. One evening, as usual, I drove my car down the gravel road to the house, got out slowly, opened the front door, and dropped my purse and briefcase in the entry hall. With my coat still on, I walked through the family room, opened the glass doors leading to the beach, and stepped out. Staring at the water against the Seattle cityscape, I took deep breaths, letting it sink in that I was now going back into normal life. It made it seem like nothing had happened. Bone tired, I thought, *Life goes on*. Standing and staring from the water's edge, I wondered, *How am I going to do this?*

I got cold while thinking about these things and turned around to go inside. Before me was a 180-degree rainbow over the house, arching from the ground on the left over the roof and down to the ground on the right.

> Hope is everything.
> —Ricky Gervais, *After Life*[13]

The radio that had come back to life after Thanksgiving blasted an alarm at 4:00 a.m. that I did not set a few weeks after the memorial service. Startled, I woke out of a sound sleep. Annoyed at the interruption yet curious about what it could mean, I said, "Okay, I'm up. Now what do you want me to do?"

I looked out the bedroom window overlooking the black, rolling, shining water overshadowed by a midnight-blue velvet sky bespeckled with white stars and a bright-yellow crescent moon. Underneath it all, I felt the force of the sun lingering behind the velvet curtain, the most magnificent night sky I had ever seen before or have since. The midnight blue was the exact shade of the 1950 Buick sedan my mother drove us around in to get groceries and the mohair yarn at The Knit Shop, her favorite home away from home.

The first time the radio returned, it played "You Are My Sunshine, please don't take my sunshine away." It turns out I was singing only the refrain, never the verse, but I was thankful for the wakeup call.

The first day back at work, my friend Dick came in, sat down, and asked me point blank, "Now what are you going to do?"

I surprised myself, bursting out with a flow of words I had no idea were in me. "I'm going to see if I can determine whether Ashley's death was an accident or destiny."

As I was answering him, a series of images, like slides, appeared before my eyes: books and films I was attracted to just prior to her leaving on the trip, the book by C. S. Lewis entitled *A Grief Observed*, a movie with Whoopi Goldberg and Ray Liotta about a housekeeper/nanny who comes to take care of a widower's little girl and helps her deal with her grief, an image of Ashley as she bade me goodbye that night before she left and I visualized what looked like a brown river on her abdomen. I still thought it so strange to have that image of what I imagined to be her digestive tract.

A hairdresser at the salon where I regularly got my hair cut had recommended *A Grief Observed*. He had lost his partner recently, and the book brought him a great deal of comfort. I immediately went to buy it. When I got it home, I thought, *I hate books on grief. I am not going to read this.* All I can say is I was compelled to buy something I normally would never read. I was equally attracted to the Whoopi Goldberg movie. When I visualized the brown river on Ashley's abdomen that night, I hadn't understood the image. I thought I was imagining her digestive tract, which made no sense. From this mind-imposed slide show, stories from the Mothers' Club (a grief group of mothers of children who had died), and the synchronous move to Bainbridge Island on September 2, two days before Ashley died, I thought in hindsight that I was being prepared for what eventually happened. I wondered if her death was part of a larger plan for her life.

A few weeks after the memorial, Mary Steele, a friend I met while studying at Antioch University, came to visit and spend the night on Bainbridge Island. Mary was the financial aid advisor who arranged several internships for me while I attended the clinical psychology program. She had a daughter the same age as Anna, and we attended lots of events together over the years with the girls.

On the way over on the ferry, we talked about all that had transpired. I told Mary, "I wish I could call Ashley on the phone and talk with her. I wish there were a phone line to heaven. It would be so great to be able to reach her by phone and have an actual conversation with her."

Minutes after we walked in the door of the house, the phone rang. I picked it up, saying, "Hello." There was no answer. I repeated, "Hello, hello, is anyone there?" No answer again. I hung up, and Mary and I began making dinner. The phone rang again. Still no answer. I began to get annoyed until Mary said, "Jane, you asked to be able to talk with Ashley on the telephone, and that's what is happening. She is calling you."

That night and for the next two nights, the phone rang with no answer. Carol Angel stayed at my house the following night, and I told her about the calls. When the phone rang while she was there, she nearly jumped out of her skin. I think she wanted to go home, but she stayed anyway. I loved the phone calls, and with Mary's help in translation, I felt connected.

Those first months, I often stayed in town with friends rather than ferry to Bainbridge Island. I was losing energy, and after a day of work, it was good to land at Mary and Doug's or

Ellen and Chris's for cozy downtime and spirited conversation, turkey tacos, and a gin and tonic with grapefruit instead of lime. During this time, I found a new affinity with appliances.

In the bedroom where I slept at her modern condo overlooking Pike Place Market, Mary had a big, white fan. She asked me to turn it on, which I tried to do, but it would not turn on. She said, "Keep trying. It should turn on. There's nothing wrong with it." She tried herself, and it began whirring and blowing.

In the morning, she loaned me her electric toothbrush. Even though it was not remote controlled and not plugged in, it started when she handed it to me. It continued to vibrate even when I turned it off. There were other instances of appliances coming on and off. Mary said, "Jane, I want you to stay away from my appliances! I don't want to have to replace them all."

Electronic appliances started unexpectedly or would not start at all when I got near them, and I came to accept these odd occurrences, which lasted for about six months.

My job provided a lifesaving structure for the day. I had to get up, take the ferry from Bainbridge Island, trudge four blocks up the hill to the office, greet friends at the firm, go to meetings, and work. This routine helped me balance by focusing on concrete assignments rather than accepting that Ashley was gone. I was good at compartmentalizing. I saved my sadness for when I got home. Staring at the fire for hours while eating Cambozola cheese and mashed potatoes for dinner, Dutch Babies for breakfast, and maple bars in between, I gained twenty pounds over nine months.

Marketing work required focusing on specific goals—business development, media relations, event management, advertising, and web content. This kind of work was perfect during the first years of grief. Right off the bat, I could connect with people socially and discuss business, although I could barely concentrate enough to read, which was a handicap.

I focused on work, covering up grief with my cheerful compartmentalization and thinking I was doing a good job. Wanting to embrace life and be more than my grief, I desperately wanted to behave in a way that would not cause people to feel sorry for me and treat me differently. A year later, our receptionist told me that by the way I behaved, she would have never known anything had happened.

I can best describe my early grief as a computer. When first learning of Ashley's death, I was a computer shut off. After a while, the screen saver came on, so it looked like the software was operating, but none of it was running. With the screen saver on, I could go back to work, have conversations, and meet individually and collectively about projects.

Beyond

From my point of view, it was impossible to see that none of the programs were up. I could pull up Word to write; however, reading was extremely challenging. I was able to negotiate with another company to put on joint seminars, but the simplest arithmetic proved difficult. I could keep going with the screen saver and intermittent Word program operating. I could read a couple of sentences in an email. If it went beyond that to more detail or another subject, I had to move on to the next one.

A few weeks went by, and I knew I would not be able to keep my job if I didn't start reading. I asked Brooke, our marketing coordinator, to sit next to me while I read a simple invitation to an event. Concentrating with every ounce of will and determination, I got through the invitation, out of breath. I managed to read it haltingly with her by my side, like a first grader who finally got it when the letters and sounds made a word and then a sentence. After that, I was able to write and read by myself. I could also slowly read documents. I thought, *Hey, I'm back at it again. Good to go. Humming along.*

Who is my neighbor? My neighbor is the one who crosses the road for me!
    —Henri Nouwen, *Bread for the Journey*[14]

Firefly

TRISHA, MY FRIEND AND NEIGHBOR, WAS THE FIRST person I asked Ellen to shepherd me to after learning Ashley had died. Both Ashley and Anna babysat for Trisha's boys over many years. Trisha was home during the day, so she kept an eye on Ashley's comings and goings after school during her teenage years. After learning Ashley was missing, Trisha called me every day for a year. Sometimes she just left a message about some crows she saw, ladybugs that landed on her, or something funny her kids said or did. The subject didn't matter, although the content was usually humorous or helpful. She was continuously present.

In addition to the Compassionate Friends group Ellen had recommended, Trisha told me literally thirteen times that I needed to see a therapist. The day I made the first appointment with a therapist named Sharon, I called Trisha and told her thirteen times, "I am going to see a therapist." Sharon was a great fit for me.

On what would have been Ashley's twenty-third birthday, February 26, six weeks after we knew she had died, Trisha made plans to bake her lemon cake with lemon icing and come home with me to Bainbridge Island. She met me after work, and in the middle of the crosswalk on our way to the ferry terminal, she told me that Ashley's cat, Carmella, had died earlier that day. Carmella, who was being cared for by the young men renting my Green Lake house, had appeared to be suffering. Trisha crossed the street and took Carmella to her veterinarian, who told her that Carmella had an acute kidney infection, and it would be best to put her to sleep. Carmella died in Trisha's arms on Ashley's birthday.

After arriving at the house, we made dinner, set the table, and included a place for Ashley. I brought out the poster-sized picture of Ashley in Ecuador that we used for the memorial and plunked it in the chair as if she were there. We heard knocking at the back door, and there were Ashley's close friends Holly and Cindy. They had decided to take the ferry to come for a visit. I left Ashley's picture in the chair and set up two more. The photograph showed Ashley in hiking clothes and a backpack. She was grinning with her curly hair wrapped up in a bun in the back. The photo looked to me like an ad in a catalog for an outdoor retailer like REI or Eddie Bauer. The great thing about the photo was that it captured her "coolness" and was huge. After everybody left, I put on music and danced with the picture all over the house, a custom that became a habit.

J. E., MY FIRST ROOMMATE AT UW, LIVED WITH HER husband, Chuck, and two grown daughters on Bainbridge Island close to where I was staying. J. E. loved extravagantly, best described as like Jesus's friend Mary who, before his last days, took an alabaster jar of oil worth a month's wages and poured it on his head. J. E. loved with a whole and complete heart. She filled her jar to overflowing with three gifts.

The first gift was introducing me to Linda G., who worked for a hospice-care company in Kitsap County and whose two sons died the prior year. Linda lived along Sunrise Drive, the same main road where I lived on Bainbridge Island. She called me to introduce herself and again on Mother's Day for support that I didn't expect or know I needed.

Finally, she invited me to join the Mothers' Club. It was made up of women of varying ages, all of whom had children who had died. Most were recent deaths. However, one mother in the group had a daughter who had died twelve years earlier. She said, "I wanted to come to the Mothers' Club tonight because I still need to go to a place where I can freely talk about my daughter, what happened to her, and not have to hold in my feelings, pretending I'm over it. It doesn't take long before people in my life do not want to hear me talk about her." It was hard to understand how her need could be so great after twelve years. Little did I know.

On Easter, J. E. called to tell me of the Good Friday service at her church. A large, rugged, wooden cross stood at the front of the church. The vicar asked each parishioner to think of deep personal suffering and gave people nails to hammer their suffering into the cross. J. E. took three nails: one for Ashley, one for Tyler, and one for me.

Beyond

ON A JULY MORNING TOWARD THE END OF MY STAY AT the Bainbridge Island house, I was getting ready to leave to catch the 7:10 a.m. ferry for work. I got a feeling I should take the 8:10 instead. Anna had arrived from Colorado and was staying with me prior to her and Steve's wedding to be held later in the month. The sun was shining as I walked toward the beach and stood on a bleached log facing the water when two deer appeared on the beach in front of me. As they walked, I turned around to see Anna getting up with her blanket wrapped around her. Motioning quietly for her to come over to the log, we stood silently watching the deer saunter gracefully, slowly down the beach.

SIX MONTHS AFTER ASHLEY'S MEMORIAL, ANNA MARRIED Steve in Seattle. The timing coincided with my need to move from Bainbridge Island back to my Green Lake home. In the two-week period before my house was vacant, I was able to stay with Vana, a sorority sister who lived in an elegant home in the Capitol Hill neighborhood. She asked me to take care of her house while she vacationed in the San Juan Islands. All I needed to do was water the plants and grass during a particularly scorching July. One night

Firefly

before her departure, she packed to leave while I moved my things from my stay at the Bainbridge Island house into her basement.

Her basement had a large recreation room with a linoleum floor of shiny beige and brown tiles with red flecks. A life-sized male dummy dressed in khakis and a red reindeer sweater sat on a beige couch along one side of the room under the window. A friend of Vana's gave it to her as a joke, and she placed it on the couch so it would look like a real man. The problem was it *did* look like a real man, especially when the lights were off. Also in the basement was a sweet, pale green-and-white guest bedroom with twin beds where Nancy and I slept the night before Anna and Steve's wedding.

Vana suggested I center my things on and around a large table in the recreation room. I had my clothes and the giant memorial picture of Ashley in her camping gear, and I set the picture in the middle of the table.

The wedding rehearsal dinner occurred the first night of my stay at Vana's. Nancy had flown in from Washington, DC, and we returned to the house from the dinner late. Nancy liked to run into bed and turn out the lights and was able to fall asleep in one minute. She did just that while I needed time to settle, so I sat with the "rubber man" on the couch. After fifteen minutes, I got up and mistakenly turned off a main switch that caused all the lights in the basement to go out. The room became black and impenetrable.

I couldn't find a light switch. Feeling along the walls with my hands, trying to get oriented, I walked around like a blind woman, inch by inch, until I stepped into something wet. There was a lot of water. It seemed as though I walked in the dark, in the wetness, for minutes, calling out to Nancy, who was out cold. I got more anxious while trying to find a light switch, worrying about my bags and boxes on the table and floor in the big room. All had been dry when I brought in my things.

At last, I found the switch, and to my immense relief, the lights came on. A large pool of water circled beneath the table where I'd placed most of my belongings. I looked around, trying to find where the water was emanating from. I thought there might be a leak in the sprinkler system and the water was finding its way into the basement. Since it was close to midnight, pitch black outside, and I was bone tired, I headed for bed instead of investigating. The next morning, the water was still on the floor.

As Nancy and I prepared to go to the wedding, I realized that I had left my ivory silk mother-of-the-bride shoes at the office. There was no time to fetch them, so I pulled a pair of bone-colored pumps from Vana's shoe collection upstairs, and we drove to the wedding. For the rest of my time at Vana's, I watched the pool of water under the table shrink and evaporate in the heat. No new water.

After Vana returned from her vacation and I moved home, she and I went to lunch at a Green Lake bistro. I told her about the water and asked her if she had ever had a problem like that in her basement before. She said, "No, I have never had anything like that happen in my house."

"Not even with the sprinklers?"

She shook her head. "No."

LADYBUGS WERE POPPING UP HERE AND THERE. TRISHA'S son, Spencer, had a birthday party in October, and a ladybug crawled up one of the candles on his cake. After Halloween, Trisha opened her garage to get something out of her car, and two dead ladybugs were on the hood. While sitting in the pew at the memorial, Marlys looked down to see a ladybug crawling along her skirt.

Because of the many ladybug appearances, Carol Angel investigated various undetermined sources as to their history and meaning. This is what she said.

> Ladybug is derived from "Our Lady's bird," named for Mary, the mother of Jesus. During the Middle Ages, ladybugs were considered sacred. For at least fifteen hundred years, farmers in Europe welcomed ladybugs on their vines, knowing they ate insect pests. Feeling thankful to these brightly colored beetles —and grateful to the mother of Jesus, who they worshiped—people called them "Beetles of Our Blessed Lady" or "Ladybirds."

Beyond

People once thought ladybugs had magical powers. In Europe, if a girl wanted a boyfriend, she would let a ladybug perch on her fingertips. She would tell it to "fly away home" and let it go, believing her boyfriend would come from wherever the ladybug flew. In early America, it was said that a ladybug would bring good luck if found in the house, especially in winter. Indeed, ladybugs are thought to bring good luck in many countries of the world. In Germany, if one flies into the house, it is believed that the family that lives there will become rich.

ON JUNE 20, 1996, TRISHA AND I FINISHED WATCHING the final concrete pour for a heavy wooden table at Green Lake that the neighbors had purchased in Ashley's name. My neighbor, J. Reich, initiated and guided the process. It had seemed right to place the memorial close to the lake that gave our neighborhood its name. We chose its place along the walking path around the lake: a grassy mound overlooking the Bathhouse Theater adjacent to the public swimming hole.

Workers told us we could place memorabilia or ashes in the concrete. We had made a bronze plaque with the inscription *Te quiero. Eris mi inspiracion*, translated as, "I love you. You are my inspiration." Ashley wrote this phrase to me in a red heart valentine stuck onto a white lace doily in high school when she was taking Spanish. As it captured how I felt about her, I sent it back to her, engraving it in bronze. On either side of the plaque, I carefully placed in the concrete the two smooth, oval, gray stones found on that early morning walk on Bainbridge Island that I had stared at, held in my hands, and slept with during the search.

Ashley Kate Palumbo
September 4, 1995
Te quiero
Eris mi inspiracion

A LARGE CROW HOPPED ONTO OUR PINK BLANKET directly in front of us, looking into our faces as the workers finished the concrete pour to lock the table in place.

The previous week, I had arranged a birthday lunch for Brooke, the young woman who worked as the marketing coordinator at the law firm. We were to meet at the Dahlia Lounge in downtown Seattle. Coincidentally, Brooke was a friend of Ashley's from her sorority and the same age. I wanted to be sure that in honoring Ashley, I was also honoring Brooke and honoring life.

After placing the plaque and stones, I raced to the Dahlia Lounge where Brooke and Len, another office friend, had already ordered salads. While talking about Brooke's birthday and the Green Lake table, a ladybug crawled out of Brooke's salad. We were all surprised to see it, especially in this lovely restaurant. The ladybug crawled onto Brooke's arm, moving this way and that, onto her hand and back up her arm, and flying away only as we walked out the door of the restaurant.

By August, I was back in my Green Lake bungalow where I had raised the girls. One morning, Mary and I took the 2.8-mile walk around Green Lake, six blocks from my home. She asked, "Now what are you going to do? Is it okay being home?"

Assuring her it was okay being home, I said, "What I really want is to get a dog." When she asked what kind of dog, I said, "Some sort of German shepherd mix."

Although I had never wanted a dog in my adult life, I longed for one now. I knew why I said I wanted a German shepherd mix. A dog had wandered to the door at the Bainbridge Island house a week or so after the memorial. It looked like a German shepherd except that it had long hair. I did not know there were long-haired German Shepherds and so thought it was a mixed breed. The dog kept looking at me with kind eyes.

I asked Sue and Richard, who lived up the road on Morning Lane, if they might know where the collarless dog belonged. They asked around the neighborhood, but no one claimed to know him. Finally, the dog disappeared. While at Sue and Richard's, one of their two Bernese Mountain Dogs walked over to me, stood on his hind legs, and placed his paws on my shoulders. Susan, who loves all animals, said, "Oh, he knows," referring to the loss of Ashley. Since then, I wanted to know about dogs and how they knew these things.

Mary and I finished our walk and returned home, continuing our conversation over tea. The living room, filled with sunlight, was warm enough that I opened the front and back doors to let in the breeze. We sipped tea and talked when a dog's head appeared, peeking into the living room from the kitchen door opening, hesitating as if saying "Hi, can I come in?"

We said, "Come on in." A brown dog of a mixed breed with no collar or identification walked across the room and laid down at my feet, remaining still and panting excessively for about five minutes. He panted so much I thought he might be sick. He got up, walked to Mary, and sat at her feet for several minutes. We looked at each other from across the room, wide eyed and dumbstruck. She said, "Maybe this dog is hungry."

I walked to the kitchen, opened the refrigerator, looked, and yelled, "All I have is cottage cheese." The brown fellow came into the kitchen, looked at the white stuff, turned up his nose, and walked out the back door to the sidewalk and down the street. I called out to Mary, "One of my kids hates cottage cheese. I can never remember which one it is." We laughed.

I never saw that dog again, and with Seattle's leash laws, random dogs are an anomaly. In thirty years of living in my house at Green Lake, no other dogs ever wandered in.

Friends Susan and David invited me to dinner at a restaurant in their Montlake neighborhood. While enjoying our meal, David asked me what I was planning to do now that I was back home. I said, "I want to take a trek in the Himalayas to know what Ashley experienced before she died. I want to stand on Indian soil. I don't want to take the exact path in India she and Tyler walked though. That would be like a death march. I'd like to take the trek they intended to take next in Nepal." It was like the question Dick asked me on the day I returned to work, "What are you going to do now?" Sometimes you don't know until someone asks the question and listens. David practically leaped across the table and said, "We will give you our miles so you can take the trip, business class."

Two days later, I received a document showing that the miles had been transferred to my name! I almost couldn't take it in. It was that fast. A week later, I contacted Nancy, and we began planning the trip. Shortly after that, while at a party on

Firefly

the opening day of boating season, I ran into Shirley, an old friend from college and a seasoned traveler. She got excited hearing about the trip, and I invited her to come with me. Thank God for Shirley. Not only did she accompany me as a friend, she handled many of the planning details that, without realizing it, I was not emotionally equipped to handle alone.

My therapist, Sharon, repeatedly suggested that I plant a tree for Ashley. I put it off for almost a year until the anniversary date of Ashley's death. Trisha and I went to a nursery in Bellevue and selected a crabapple tree called Purple Prince for its shiny, purplish bark and magenta blossoms. We chose a crabapple so that it would not interfere with the wires over my house. We joked that Ashley would rather have had a Himalayan hemlock, one of the tallest, stateliest trees in the Northwest, because she had always wanted to be tall. Instead, we picked a short, cute one for utilitarian and aesthetic reasons.

The week before we planted it, I asked Ashley to please communicate to me what her last day was like. I asked because I didn't know anything, wasn't there, and wanted help with understanding. I had no idea if I would experience understanding, and I became fearful that if I did get an answer, I would feel like I was drowning and would not be able to breathe.

Beyond

Trisha, Spencer, Anna, and I got up early to walk around Green Lake. When we got home, we walked to the front lawn where Trisha's husband, Peter, had dug a deep hole in the corner of the grass beyond the white picket fence surrounding the front yard. To that point, I felt normal but concerned that the drowning feeling might come on soon. The moment we put the tree in the earth and began shoveling brown clods under and around it, joy surged from inside of me, filling every bit of body space, starting from my stomach and pushing out through my arms and legs, fingers and toes—big, virtually uncontainable joy.

The little crabapple continues to grow and thrive outside the front picture window. It looks like one of those trees you draw when you are a child: a big, brown trunk with a round, green top. It made me feel better when I looked at it to know it was growing. We put something back into the earth that grows stronger and sturdier and grander for its short stature every day.

> It is only after the deepest darkness that the greatest joy can come.
>
> —Malcolm X[15]

Journey

Nancy

When I returned to Kathmandu after the memorial in Seattle, it was still hard to accept that Ashley had died. I went to work but remained unfocused. I wanted to be closer to Jane and worried about her, although I knew she had many friends and Anna at her side. Back in Nepal, I still hoped in some strange way that Ashley would appear one day. I looked at every young, dark-haired tourist couple to see if they could be Ashley and Tyler.

Not long after I returned, Jane called to say that she knew that she wanted to come to Nepal for a trek. She hoped that by being in the Himalayas she could understand more what drove Ashley to travel so far on such an adventure.

I selected a location for the trek that wouldn't be too challenging and with guides I thought would be responsible and sensitive to our needs. I knew it would be an emotional experience.

Prior to leaving on the trip to India and Nepal, Sharon told me, "If you feel drawn or pulled toward anything, follow it."

Wearing black leather clogs, I put my feet on the ground of the country where Ashley last walked, took a tour of the

Taj Mahal, and got the hell out of there to Nepal. As the plane took off from Delhi for the flight to Kathmandu, tears rolled down my face. I was never so glad to get out of a place. I never wore the clogs again but stored them in my basement until moving out thirteen years later.

Upon landing in Kathmandu, Nancy greeted Shirley and me. She held in her hands two white, gauzy scarves that had been blessed by the local Buddhist priest. She wrapped the scarves around our necks and whisked us away to her cozy home nearby.

Nancy had arranged for us to go on a weeklong trek in the foothills of the Annapurna range in the Himalayas. We stayed in teahouses, and it was a long, rocky trail amidst mountain peaks and terraced farmland. It was so rocky that our guide offered to trade his boots with me, since mine were low-tops and his were high-tops, which gave considerably more support for the uneven terrain. Luckily, he and I wore the same size.

It was magical in the Himalayas. We sat outside on rocks drinking hot, sweet Nepali chai with milk and spices in the cool, crisp air with the sun at our backs. Tibetan burros in full red-and-gold regalia trotted down the mountain past us. Nepalese men and women we passed on the trail greeted us with "Namaste," heads bowed and hands folded. I call it magical too because in every photograph, each of us looked fifteen to twenty years younger.

I had been told over and over that it was important to "let go" for Ashley's sake so that she could move on and not be obliged to hang around me until I was okay. The first sunset of the trek, I left the group with our guide who walked me to the river. I set up camp for my goodbye ceremony with a book of matches and a candle. I told him my plan and that I needed to find two small rocks, one for Ashley and one for Tyler, to throw into the river to symbolize for Ashley that I was letting her go. Holding up two small, gray, heart-shaped stones with white, horizontal stripes, the guide asked me, "Will these work?"

I couldn't believe they were heart shaped. "They're perfect."

He handed them to me and walked back to the teahouse where the others were getting settled for bed. I found a few other ordinary stones that were smooth and put them in my pocket.

As the sun lowered, I sat square on the boulder's face and prepared my speech to Ashley. Looking into the sun's last rays as it set on the river, I lit a candle and told her, "I'm letting you go. Go on ahead. You can move on and do whatever it is you need to do now. You don't have to take care of me. I'll be fine." I threw the ordinary stones into the river and kept the heart-shaped ones in my hand.

Beyond

WE CONTINUED OUR TREK THROUGH GREEN AND YELLOW rice fields alongside jutting mountain peaks on rocky terrain. We stopped often at teahouses along the way for meals of dal bhat, a dish of lentils, rice, and vegetables with tiny potatoes, and more Nepali tea. Along the path, we encountered a group of men: one from the UK, one from Australia, and another from New Zealand. They called us the sixties chicks and made for lively companions on the way to the top at Poon Hill where we all stayed in a cobalt-blue teahouse for dinner and overnight lodging. The next morning at 4:00 a.m., we were scheduled to hike with headlamps to an elevation of 10,531 feet to reach Poon Hill to watch the sunrise over the Annapurna range.

Nancy took the lead and urged me as we got higher. "Hurry up, Jane. You need to pick up the pace, or you'll miss the sunrise." I was nauseated from the altitude and had trouble breathing. I had diarrhea. My worst fear before I'd embarked on this adventure was that I'd have diarrhea, no bathroom, and a bunch of people all around. Now I not only had diarrhea but also felt like throwing up.

One foot in front of the other at a turtle's pace, I managed to make it to the top just before sunrise. While the other trekkers were watching the sun come up over the mountains, I sat behind them in the tall, yellow grass, taking care of business and laughing at myself. It turned out that my worst fear was not such a big deal after all. From my stance in the grass, I watched the bold, white sunlight silhouetting the jagged peaks of the Annapurna range. It was the third-most beautiful experience of my life after the births of Anna and Ashley.

With the spectacle of the Poon Hill vista on our minds, we began our descent surrounded by jagged, snow-covered peaks and a royal-blue sky. Halfway down the mountain, Nancy signaled to the Nepali guide who carried bright green, red, yellow, and blue prayer flags. Each flag displayed Tibetan script bearing prayers that were said to sprinkle on the wind when hung. We stretched the colorful squares of cloth across two large sticks in the ground facing the mountains directly in front of us. They were hung alongside other flags, as Nancy indicated the ground we stood on was a place of honoring. The Nepalese people had flown flags for hundreds of years in memory of their dead, and our prayers for Ashley and Tyler were scattered along with the others.

This was the culmination of the trek Nancy had originally planned for them.

Prayer Flags

Nancy

I asked the guide to help us find prayer flags, as I had forgotten to bring them. Each flag had the Buddhist prayer "Om Mani Padme Hum" on it written in Tibetan—I can't remember what that means, but they are ancient, sacred words. They are powerful, and I knew we needed them. The guide, who had walked as many miles as we had, happily ran down the trail and came back with the colorful flags. We were able to hang them and take an iconic panoramic photo of Jane and the flags with the Himalayas in the background.

WE HIKED DOWN FROM THE POON HILL STATION AND took a bus to Pokhara for a break after the trek. It was evening when we reached this charming village surrounded by stalky golden marigolds. They were like golden balls on sticks. Nancy showed us around the town and pointed out various shops, including clothing, souvenir, and jewelry stores. Worn out, we had our dinner of dal bhat and went to bed.

The next morning, I woke up restless. I remembered that before I left for India, Sharon had counseled me that if I felt an attraction toward anything at all, I should follow it. After breakfast, we started looking around at the clothes hanging outside in the courtyard. I grew restless to the point of being irritable. I didn't want to be looking at clothes, and I declared emphatically and uncharacteristic of my easy-going nature, "I'm going in that jewelry store way over on the left." I could hardly wait to get there, having no patience for deciding what activity to do next. There was a kind of urgency about the feeling.

Making a beeline to the store, I burst in and looked at the jewelry in the glass case: lovely stones in unusual combinations displayed in neat rows. I gazed at the rings until my eyes focused on one with a smooth, opaque-white moonstone surrounded by tiny, sparkling emeralds and rubies, alternating every other one. The white, red, and green stones from Ashley's dream appeared clear across the world in a ring I had been seeking for her for years. Losing all composure, I hid in the corner of the store and cried.

Nancy walked in and found me. "What's going on?"

I told her between gulps and tears about the search for the ring, and she put it together. I said, "I don't know what to do. It was supposed to be Ashley's ring, not mine. I don't know what I should do."

She was emphatic. "Buy the ring."

It was clear to her what I needed to do, but I didn't like people telling me what to do unless I was unhinged and wrecked, which I was. Nancy took over and made the transaction with the shopkeeper. I looked at the ring on my hand, simultaneously confused and finished with whatever I was supposed to do on this trip. It felt like a closing, a kind of ending.

Having completed our journey, we took the daylong bus ride back down to Kathmandu. I was uncomfortable wearing the ring on my hand, disturbing because it was supposed to be Ashley's. As if the excursion in the Himalayas was not enough, Nancy walked me to a cozy carpet store called Pema Chodron where we sipped sweet Nepali tea and contemplated the thick, wool Tibetan rugs in patterns ranging from walking tigers to Buddhist symbols in various sizes and colors. I planned to carpet every square inch of my house with these rugs, surrounding myself with "essence of Ashley." I would have eaten those rugs if I could, and I bought as many as I could afford: a deep-blue one with white cranes, another with light-brown and pale-blue Buddhist symbols, and two little ones with maroon, green, and pink stripes and crosses. The colors of the soft Tibetan wool promised comfort I could wrap myself in and on. Satisfied, I took my last sip of tea.

Firefly

SOME YEARS ARE TURNING POINTS. THAT FIRST YEAR, 1996, which included my time at Bainbridge Island, Ashley's disappearance and death, and the end of the search for her, began my search for a way to go on living prayerfully, joyfully. It was also the year of a harvest gold moon touching the water in my backyard, the full rainbow arcing over the house to greet me on my return home from work, and shiny, black-and-white Orca whales sidling up against the white ferry like pets. Otters scurrying across the back lawn, deer getting into the garbage cans and later walking side by side on the beach, and eagles circling overhead. I heard in a simple sermon at Grace Episcopal Church, "Where do you find God? In the dirt and wherever bread is broken." The vicar threw dirt in the aisle to make his point. I was welcomed home to Bob Dylan's "The Times They Are A-Changin'" playing in my empty house near Green Lake. My eleven-year-old friend and neighbor, Spencer, gave me all his stuffed animals to sleep with when I visited the old neighborhood on Halloween and then gave me a white stuffed bear to take home. That same year, Carmella, Ashley's fluffy, gray tabby, died on Ashley's birthday, six weeks after we learned she had drowned. It was the support of the monthly meeting of the Mothers' Club with others in mourning, exchanging cookies, friendship, and stories of amazing, otherworldly occurrences in the safe harbor of Sunrise Drive on Bainbridge Island down the street from my temporary home on Morning Lane.

How was it that 1996, when for the first time in twenty-one years I left my Green Lake home to spend a year on Bainbridge Island with its bountiful natural beauty, could coincide with Ashley's death? I believed at the time I was being held and comforted for something horribly inevitable. I couldn't be sure of it, but that was what I was coming to believe, and I was not one of the people who thought there was a reason for everything.

New Chapters

"The house symbolizes the self." I heard that on NPR, and perhaps it explained why I'd always been attracted to small houses, cottages, and cabins. For me, they were sturdy, simple, strong, welcoming structures that spelled cozy comfort in gentle lights.

The robin's egg-blue house, a Sears catalog-style bungalow set on a bare postage stamp of a lawn, welcomed me when I met it, even with its aqua-blue asbestos siding and generic white trim. When I bought the Green Lake house in 1975, Anna was five years old and Ashley was two.

Two years later, the house transformed into an eggshell-sheened hunter green with shiny, battleship-gray trim. My carpenter/artist boyfriend removed the toxic asbestos exterior to restore the original wood. The house emerged from its siding like a thing of simple beauty, appearing like a large, wooden boat poised to sail across the small front lawn bordered by a cement sidewalk. When the old wood siding pulsed to breathe, the green paint cracked and split after seven years, just like him.

The next color transformed the dark-green sailing ship into Wedgewood blue with dove-gray trim. It remained that basic blue for years; I never tired of it. I changed the front door from purple eggplant to peach and finally to a bright, "Happy Day" yellow. My favorite, and the favorite of my neighbors, the eggplant color, stayed on the longest. Dear Trisha got mad when I painted it peach.

Ashley died, and I came home from my sabbatical and the good life of Bainbridge Island. Time to paint the house again, and this time I chose a sage green-gray combination. I chose the colors for their hues and in large part because of the manufacturer's names: Rushing River for the base, White Heron for the warm white trim, and Raisin for the interior window and door trims. The Raisin looked almost black on the paint swatch, so I dismissed it because I didn't like black on my house. It was too final. A second look, pointed out by an interior designer down the block, revealed the black to be a deep, dark maroon I could use for the doors and windows, the ways in and out. In the sunlight, the true warm tone inside the Raisin emerged, and I came home and painted myself in.

Mary swooped in two weeks after I moved back into the house. She brought along a group of friends and family to repaint the interior with hues of gold and pale apricot, colors of the sunrise and sunset. I felt warmed by the colors and the visual of these old friends painting the walls, laughing, rolling, and brushing clean warmth on every square inch.

ABOUT A YEAR AFTER ASHLEY'S DEATH, RANDY, THE KINDest six-foot-five boss I've ever had, called me into his office and said gently, "Jane, your performance is not up to the level it needs to be. You need to step it up to keep your job."

As I sat behind the round table opposite his big, solid walnut desk, I listened to him talk as if I were walled off behind something. It was hard to explain. I could hear him talk, and I knew he wanted me to improve my performance. Had he not told me, I would not have known I wasn't performing well—I thought my compartmentalization had been working. Besides feeling a buzzing all over, gazing out the window of his fortieth-floor office in the Seattle City Centre Building as he explained more, it began to feel as though a quarter-inch-thick glass wall emerged between us. I felt badly that I was doing all I could but it was not good enough. I knew as I sat there that there was no way I could make myself perform any better.

Firefly

Embarrassed and disoriented, I walked slowly back to my office. In shattering the denial, the confrontation thrust me into reality. Terrified that I would lose my job and knowing I couldn't step it up under my own power, I sat on my chair, facing the blank wall, and prayed hard. I have since learned that the type of problem I was having is called lack of executive function of the brain. In this case, literally and figuratively, I lacked executive function.

I KNEW I NEEDED TO FIND A CHURCH TO ATTEND EVERY week. No more intermittent attendance during crisis times. I wanted what church consistently provided for me: comfort and hope through a steady perspective that there was a larger reality than what I could see. I scoped out the churches in the University District, which was down the hill and about five minutes' drive from home. I knew that whatever church I chose, it would have to be easy to get to so I could fall out of bed and roll down the hill.

During the week, I spotted a small Episcopal church, the sign reading that the service started at 9:30 a.m. Sunday morning. I decided to attend. As planned, the following Sunday, I got out of bed, dressed, and rolled down the hill to the church, arriving at 9:25. People were filing out. Confused, I asked a parishioner, "What's happening? The sign says services start at 9:30."

A woman replied matter-of-factly, "Oh, it's summer. The service time changed. They must not have changed the sign."

I was disappointed, as I had carefully determined that this was the church I wanted. I had attended Episcopalian services at Saint Mark's Episcopal Cathedral, the beautiful, immense structure where Anna and Ashley were baptized and Ashley and Tyler's memorial took place. However, I felt the need for a cozy, snug church, more like a blanket I could wrap myself into. My other requirement was that the church needed to be as intellectual as it was spiritual.

Since I was already dressed up, I was determined to go to any church, no matter what, at least that Sunday (I hated getting dressed formally on the weekend after wearing suits and dresses at the law firm all week). That way, I could look into other options. After all, I was on a hunt for a cozier church than a cathedral. I thought, *I'll check out University Congregational, where I worshiped in college.* It was a few blocks away.

Once again, scores of people were descending the stairs. "When is the next service?" I asked a woman on her way out.

She replied, "There's only one service during the summer."

Foiled again! Still determined not to let my Sunday clothes go to waste, I walked next door to the Presbyterian church. Having visited there a few times with a family friend, I remembered they had four to five services on Sundays. I thought, *They must have at least two, even if it is summer.* Sure enough, although one service was letting out, another was about to begin in half an hour. *Damn it, I'm dressed up, and I'm going to church come hell or high water, even if it is Presbyterian.* It had about three thousand total members, and although I was raised Presbyterian and it was a good experience, I didn't want to go there. I preferred the ritual of high church.

I picked a spot near the back. Everything was familiar: the hymns, the order of the service. There were a lot of people in a large space. I'd heard about the minister, Earl Palmer, for years but never listened to him speak. His sermon covered the history of the German church during World War II and how educational, scientific, governmental, and health institutions ended up capitulating to Hitler except for the Confessing Church, a declaration by Lutheran and evangelical pastors and theologians that they would not have their churches co-opted by the Nazi government for propagandistic purposes. They operated underground. Palmer's topic was so large that he couldn't cover it in one sermon, and he said he would be speaking for four consecutive Sundays about the history, politics, and the church's role in its resistance to the Nazi regime. Enthralled by the topic, I thought, *Well, I'll come back until this sermon series is over.* I wanted to know how people in the church summoned the courage to resist such pervasive evil in spite of the fact that the other institutions caved. University Presbyterian more than satisfied my intellectual requirement.

I came back for the next three sessions, and each sermon was as fascinating as the one preceding it. When the last session concluded, sitting in the pew, I thought, *Well, now what?* I loved the sermons, and they were feeding me intellectually and spiritually. I realized I was getting exactly what I needed and said to myself, *I might as well stay here, even if it is Presbyterian and huge.* Once I made the decision, I felt a sense of peace. The words "this is the place" flew into my consciousness. Ashley had said "this is the place," twice when she took me there to church on Christmas Eve. The recollection astounded me and confirmed my decision. That place, our place, became a major focus of my life for the next twenty years.

After attending church each Sunday, two years of therapy with Sharon, weekly lunches with Jane Langer, overnights, dinners, and coffees with friends, I decided that I was pretty well healed. I could help others with their grief. Years before doing marketing, I had worked as a counselor, so my new home church was happy to take me on as cofacilitator for its grief classes. I became ordained as a deacon. For a time, working in the role fed the need I had to work more directly in what I called a "God job." All along, I was trying to determine if there was life after death and if Ashley's death was fated.

I MET JANE LANGER WHEN WE WORKED AS SECRETARIES for some nice men who owned and managed shopping centers in the Pacific Northwest. After I moved back home to Green

Firefly

Lake, she called me every week to invite me to lunch.

At first, we met at the famous brass pig at Pike Place Market and pointed ourselves east to survey the numerous restaurants. Copacabana, a family-owned Bolivian restaurant, was the first one we chose. To get there, we climbed the winding, black, wrought iron stairs to its terrace overlooking shops below. Freshly planted flowers of the season lined the terrace: red, purple, and yellow petunias crammed to overflowing in the summer and dwarf evergreens with red, green, and white Christmas tree lights during winter. We decided to meet at Copacabana every time.

Smiling Bolivian women greeted us and took our orders for the same dishes each week: chicken salad with humita, corn pie with green sauce for me, and black bean soup or vegetarian salad for Jane. On our birthdays, we added arroz con leche (rice pudding).

Each table had a small, square white tablecloth embroidered with people in colorful costumes. From our perch above the shops, we spied locals and tourists strolling the cobblestone street below, selecting fresh fruit and vegetables, crab, and croissants. On a sunny day, we could see snow on top of the Olympic Mountains.

Jane kept inviting me to our lunches even though I didn't reciprocate. I was a total receptor, and she was a total giver. I told her everything that struck me as a sign, because she could handle everything as she walked with me through

Ashley's death and every piece of magic that transpired. While I tried to apply the scientific method and determine if these bits of magic were real, she smiled and said gently, the few times she could get a word in edgewise, "I just like to enjoy when these things happen."

The comfort of her continual invitations, our regular meetings, and her friendship helped nourish me during the aftermath. Toward the end of the time when we met weekly, she offered me a pale-green hardback book with lavender letters on the spine. It was a story by Rumer Godden called *An Episode of Sparrows*. I asked her why, and she smiled. "It's just a nice story I think you would like."

I did like the story and didn't want it to end, so I didn't finish it.

> But the grandest symphonic moment was a delicate sound, almost inaudible in its subtlety. It began with a tap, and gave way to a beak…and a chirp. It was the sound of life softly renewed-unwrinkled and unblemished. It was the sound of hope.
> —Charles van Sandwyk, *Mr. Rabbit's Symphony of Nature and Other Tails*[16]

On June 7, 1998, Anna and Steve's baby, Ryan, was born in South Bend, Indiana. While Steve attended business school at Notre Dame, Anna embarked on education courses at University of Indiana. On my previous visit on Easter, they took me on a walk around a lake on the Notre Dame campus. Because of its three-mile circumference and surrounding lushy evergreen foliage, I said, "This is so much like home, walking around Green Lake."

Anna corrected me. "Oh no, Mom, it's different. You'll see."

We walked along the path, and the Stations of the Cross appeared off to the side. Farther along, we came upon a statue of Saint Francis. Still farther, other saints stood erect like soldiers on the trail. She instructed me to walk up a narrow dirt path from the lake and keep following it. I walked by myself up the path into a woodsy enclosure where I encountered life-sized, bronze sculptures of Jesus on the cross with the two thieves who were crucified beside him. Mary, the mother of Jesus, and Mary Magdalene stood close to Jesus. I was floored by the massive sculptures—the literal unexpected experience of Easter.

The encounter with the crucifixion sculptures and being at Notre Dame became the backdrop of Ryan's birth. To add to the Notre Dame lore, the day Ryan was born, Steve continuously watched *Rudy*, a movie about a young man striving to become a Notre Dame football player. I watched it too, reveling in its theme of all-in enthusiasm, love, and persevering commitment. Looking at Ryan wrapped in his soft, yellow receiving blanket, I committed to life again. It was the first time since Ashley died that I felt myself sit up straight and reinvest for the long ride. I looked at his small face wriggling inside the blanket and said, "I'm going to be *all* there for you, baby, complete and totally *all* there."

I gazed out Steve and Anna's apartment balcony where a few nights earlier Steve and I had smoked cigars to celebrate Ryan's birth. It was time to go back to Seattle, and I looked down from the deck to see little, brown bunnies hopping over the red rock and grass of their front yard.

As we loaded my bags into the car for the ride to the airport, I asked to take one last look at the Grotto of Our Lady O Lourdes, a rock cave at Notre Dame's entrance guarded by a life-sized statue of Mary and with hundreds of places to light candles inside and pray. We arrived at twelve o'clock in the afternoon. The interior of the Grotto burst bright, white light as if every candle in the cave were lit. Anna and I lit candles for Ryan and for Ashley, and then she and Steve drove me to the airport.

While boarding, I looked for my seat by the window near the middle of the plane over the wing. Sitting down, I gazed out, taking in the miracle of my first grandchild's birth and the bounty of love shared by family and friends. Thinking of Ashley, I wondered if she was present, wished that she was, longed for her to be. Relishing in the memories, I turned away from the window toward the people coming down the aisle. I fixed my gaze on a short, solidly built, middle-aged woman carrying several large, colorful cloth bags. I thought, *Please don't let her sit next to me!* I wondered why I had such a strong feeling.

Sure enough, she sat in the seat next to mine and said, "Hello." We spoke a few niceties before she asked me what I had been doing in South Bend. I told her of the birth of my grandson, whereupon she cracked a great big smile, wrinkling her almost-black eyes. I realized that she looked like an older, wrinkly version of Ashley, with the same smile and flinty, sparkly eyes. She followed her smile with a pronouncement delivered slowly and deliberately. "Things have been bad. Now they will be good."

I rode her words, unexpected and providential, from bad to good and wondered how she could know what she was saying.

Arriving home late that night, I did not look at my mail. When I got home from work the next day, I found a box of checks addressed to Ashley in my mailbox. It had been nearly three years since she had died. It was amazing that these checks were sent at the same time as Ryan's birth and when I needed to know that she knew about his birth and was present. The following day, I checked in person with the bank. The woman I spoke with said, "I have no idea how these checks got sent or who sent them." I felt that Ashley was somehow with us. Another flicker of her light.

Beyond

> The boundlessness of love is made evident when the veils between this world and the invisible world are thinnest. At birth and death, love melts any division.
> —Frank Ostaseski, *The Five Invitations: Discovering What Death Can Teach Us About Living Fully*[17]

ANNA AND STEVE MOVED TO SEATTLE IN SPRING OF 2000, a month before my granddaughter Madison Ashley was born on April 20. Along with family, nature welcomed her with pink cherry blossoms bursting in front of Anna and Steve's white house. The blossoms were so abundant you could barely glimpse the sky through the upstairs windows.

Gracyn Mae entered the world on July 23, 2003. With hair the color of sunshine, she was greeted enthusiastically by her brother and sister who played in the grass outside of Anna and Steve's new house. It would not be long before she too would join them to play, jumping on the trampoline in the backyard and swimming in the pool across the street.

My grandchildren – I look at them in wonder.
They take my breath away.
The Moth Radio Hour, August 23, 2021[18]

Firefly

REDFORD, THE RED STANDARD POODLE, CAME INTO MY life, flown in from Morristown, Florida. My longing for a dog had continued no matter how hard I tried to tamp it down. Redford arrived in a small crate with a turquoise stuffed koala bear and a rumpled pig's ear. Ryan, Madison, and Anna, who was then seven months' pregnant with a broken foot, drove with me to meet Redford at the Delta terminal at Sea-Tac.

I had been yearning for a dog for years, spurred on by Anna filling her life with babies and my thought that dogs could communicate nonverbally and telepathically. I thought that loving and being with a dog might help me communicate with Ashley in my never-ending quest to stay connected to her.

Redford was so smart that he had to wait for me to catch up in our obedience training classes. I had to go over the moves several times while he learned the maneuvers correctly the first time. I chose a poodle because poodles are smart, good with children, don't shed, and have curly hair.

He and I hung out a lot at home, in the park, and on the neighborhood streets. Anna asked me how it was being around Redford. I said, "Redford is a great dog, and I love him, but he doesn't talk, and it turns out he isn't Ashley." This was a disappointment. He also gobbled dead crows and anything made of paper.

Beyond

FOURTEEN YEARS AFTER ASHLEY DIED, I DECIDED TO SELL the Green Lake home where I had lived for thirty-three years. The process of getting the house ready took one month, and I cosmetically transformed it into the best it could be without spending a fortune to remodel the kitchen and replace the furnace. Sometime over the years, I had put in a white picket fence to frame the front and a six-foot-tall cedar fence in back for Redford. How I missed Redford, who died four years earlier. He always looked me right in the eyes.

I prayed that a family would buy the house and fill it—a loving couple with children who would play, laugh, and climb in Ashley's Purple Prince crabapple tree. I had thought I could never sell the house because we planted that tree in the front yard. I loved watching it grow from a spindly, sparsely leaved creature into a thick-trunked, plump, round beauty, welcoming neighbors passing by. In April, the tree filled with magenta flowers just before the inedible maroon crabapples appeared in May. After the leaves fell in the fall, I'd hang a large, fake, feathery bird from Display and Costume Supply to surprise people as they walked by.

I still had the heart-shaped rocks that I couldn't let go of in Nepal. They had lived on my fireplace mantel ever since the trip. After putting the house on the market, it was time to let them go. I found a place in the soil underneath the front window but couldn't bear the thought of burying them. They were too pretty, so I placed them face up on the dirt adjacent to the picture window facing Ashley's tree and the street.

I moved to Janet's condo in Pioneer Square until I could find a new place to live. It was a summer of in-between, then-and-now life leading to a condo I rented in Ballard, a neighborhood west of the old one and closer to the Olympic Mountains. There was a fireplace angled like in the Green Lake house. Nancy said, "No wonder you like it. It's a miniature replica of your old house."

The Green Lake house sold two hours after it went on the market to the Olsons, a storybook Scandinavian family with parents and three little boys. The Olsons populated the front porch with strollers, bikes, and trikes and the front yard with balls of all colors and kinds. There was a Little Tyke cabin house and small and large trucks and cars strewn under Ashley's tree where Gracyn had liked to climb. "Look at me, Grandma," Gracyn would shout while twirling over and over the lowest branches. Now it was strong enough for the Olson boys to perch from a platform they built on the upper branches.

The Olsons restored the house, extending and renovating the kitchen. They improved the upstairs heating so that the older boys could play in their bedrooms. I know about the changes because in the first year, Mrs. Olson contacted me to inquire about the paint colors I had used on the outside of the house. They planned on doing some more remodeling and needed to touch up. She offered to take me on a tour of the house to see the changes. Funny thing, I was as good about the changes as if I had made them myself.

I released the house at a good time, doing all I could do to make it its best self, and then they took over. Even their antique oak furniture and L-shaped beige couch were what I would have chosen.

Talking with Mrs. Olson upstairs, the boys playing nearby, she told me she was pregnant again. This would be their fourth child, and she revealed that after I left that morning, they were going to the doctor to find out if it was a boy or a girl. I was surprised and wondered how they would be able to fit in the house with all those boys, a golden retriever, and an older, mixed, black-and-gray Lab. They would still have the basement—where Anna and Ashley had played school, dressed up in all manner of costumes and wigs to produce endless plays and musical shows—to remodel.

Mrs. Olson said, "When I found out I was pregnant again, lots of people thought we should move." As we looked out the window, she said, "Aside from really liking the house, I love its position on the street. I love watching the neighbors walk by and how it is situated on the block."

I thought, *She loves this house, its place in space and time. So do I, and I love that this beautiful family is here.*

Firefly

Months later as I drove past the house, taking the shortcut on my way to church, the Olsons had a sign on the door welcoming a baby boy just in time for Thanksgiving. I thought, *From Ashes to Olsons. Brunettes to blondes. Irish Italians to Scandinavians. Girls to boys. It's all good.*

I CONTINUED TO WRITE AT MY FRESHLY PAINTED MAROON desk at the entrance of my new condo in Ballard, and I hung Ashley's giant memorial photograph at one side of the desk. On the opposite wall, I hung an equally giant poster of Mary catching Jesus falling from the cross. Needless to say, this arrangement at the entry may have been unsettling for the people coming to visit, but I needed them both in front of me. I loved seeing Ashley's smile as I walked in the door, her backpack balanced easily with her fingers wrapped around the black straps, her gold amethyst birthstone ring on one hand and my grandmother Lola Scaife's wedding ring on the other. I could look to the opposite wall at Mary's face where I could see how I felt.

Seven years later, I moved Ashley's photo from the entry to a less front-and-center place in my bedroom. I hung it across from my bed, so she was the first person I saw when waking in the morning and the last person I saw as I went to sleep. I brought the poster of Mary and Jesus along with her. Rather than hanging it, I leaned it against the wall at the foot of the bed. It was no longer necessary to look at Mary simultaneously. She had fulfilled her purpose in companioning me, showing me how I felt.

I kept up a conversation with Ashley about all the normal things one talks to a live person about: what to make for dinner, what to watch on television, and consulting her on decisions. It was pretty much a running dialogue. It wasn't like I expected an answer—I just wanted to keep the connection.

Firefly

Drought Days

> On the long, drought days
> When I don't hear from you
> I pretend you're there,
> And maybe you are.
>
> I open my mouth to start the monologue,
> and when I've spoken
> I listen for your answer.
>
> By now I'm used to your silence.
> I don't expect to hear your voice.
> But I like to keep the conversation going.
> I pretend you're there,
> And maybe you are.
>
> —J. A.

Time passed, and in 2010, my old friend Jane Langer and I became writing partners, calling ourselves The Janes Writing Group. We began each Wednesday afternoon session by lighting a candle held in an emerald-green glass etched with a cross. As green light flickered, we prayed for friends and family while seated comfortably in champagne satin wingback armchairs in the family room of Jane's yellow house.

After our ritual, we wrote and read what we wrote for the rest of the afternoon until four o'clock.

One sunny afternoon in the fall, while we wrote, we heard a loud bang against the sliding glass door facing her patio garden. Jane hopped up and slid the door open to find a green-breasted bird lying on the cement step. She said, "I'm not sure if the bird is dead or merely stunned. Sometimes birds can revive. Let's leave it on the step to rest. We'll know in a while if it's dead."

Picking up our pens again, we wrote for a couple more hours until she put down her yellow legal pad and went to the patio to check on the bird. Sliding the door open, she gazed down and touched it. "The bird is dead."

"What do we do?" I asked.

Gently and matter-of-factly, she said, "Now that we know the bird is dead, we can bury it."

I watched as she retrieved a shovel that was leaning against the fence. We chose a burial plot between two geraniums along the border of her flowerbed next to the house. She said, "I'll dig a hole. Find some dry grass to make a nest for the bird to lay in."

I gathered grasses and placed them carefully in the hole. She scooped up the bird, holding it out to me. "Would you like to touch it?" she asked softly.

Startled at the offer, I stared into her kind face. Trembling as she moved her hand in my direction, I lightly touched the bird's soft, feathery breast with one finger.

As we moved through the burial, time slowed, and I felt myself suspended. Jane placed the lovely creature gently into the nest we had made, covered it with leaves and dirt, and carefully patted it down. She placed a flower on the grave, crossed two twigs for a marker, and said a prayer.

"We just buried Ashley," I told Jane.

"I don't understand."

"We waited all afternoon to see if the bird was dead and buried it only when we were sure. We waited for four months when Ashley was missing before we found out that she had died. Although we had a memorial service, we couldn't care for her body because she was not found. Today, the bird took her place as we prepared a nest in the earth to finally honor her small, sweet body.

"Thank you, dear bird. Thank you, Jane."

September 4, 2011

Just as Trisha always celebrated Ashley's birthday, we also celebrated hers. Unfortunately, Trisha's birthday, September 4, became the date of Ashley's death as well. In the first years after Ashley died, we split the day. In the first half of the day, we walked Green Lake and planted or placed flowers at Ashley's table. During the second half, we celebrated Trisha's birthday.

Beyond

On September 4, 2011, and for weeks preceding it, Trisha's sister was suffering from a rare lung disease caused by a bird. She was hospitalized, and Trisha was afraid her sister might die. I told her, "This year, we will celebrate your birthday *only*. I'll make lunch for us and meet you at Ashley's table. Do *not* bring anything."

A tall elm arced over the table, and the sun shone on the grassy mound where the table rested. I brought sandwiches, cookies, and tea and set our lunch on a tablecloth with china dishes, silverware, and flowers.

Trisha arrived carrying long-stemmed red roses and laid them next to the bronze plaque. She also brought me a necklace she had made with a two-inch-long teardrop pearl on a gold chain. She was a jewelry artist, often bringing me a piece of jewelry on special occasions. As always, we reminisced about how Ashley would walk across the street early in the morning to bead with her until late afternoon. I said, "Trisha, we're celebrating your birthday, not Ashley!" She ignored me.

While we ate lunch, she told me more about how dire her sister's condition was and that family was with her around the clock. They were not sure she was going to make it.

At the same time Trisha's sister was suffering, my stepmother Doris was hospitalized for an endoscopy. She had been having serious trouble breathing, and this procedure was risky given her health and age (over eighty-five). I visited her in the ICU on September 6, two days after the lunch with

Trisha. An ICU nurse worked in the room while I waited for Doris to come out of the anesthetic.

As Doris started to come out, she said, "Thank Trisha for me."

Confused, I asked, "What did you say?"

"I said thank Trisha for me."

I asked again, "What do you mean?"

"Thank her for the flowers."

Reality shifted. Doris had met Trisha once at Anna's wedding shower in 1996, fifteen years ago. I didn't know how, but I felt I was talking to someone other than Doris and that it had to be Ashley. "Please tell me what happened."

"It was just like it said in the paper. I fell in, and Tyler came in after me." After a pause, she said, "Trisha's sister will be okay, and so will Doris."

Doris awoke to full consciousness. The conversation ended, and I greeted her. I was wearing the teardrop pearl necklace Trisha had just given me. I said, "Doris, Trisha made this necklace, and I think it's for you." I put it around her neck. She smiled and thanked me without asking who Trisha was.

The ICU nurse asked me, "Do you go to University Presbyterian Church? Aren't you active there? I attend there."

Surprised, I said, "Yes, I'm a deacon there."

She began telling me about a family member she was extremely worried about and asked, "Will you pray for him?"

Astonished, I said, "Yes." The nurse, Doris, and I joined hands and prayed for her beloved family member.

At some point, another hospital employee entered the room and said to Doris, "What a beautiful necklace you're wearing."

Doris said, "My granddaughter gave it to me."

More than three thousand people attended University Presbyterian Church, which held four services each Sunday. I had never seen Doris's ICU nurse at the church or anywhere else until weeks later at a coffee hour. As I sat at a table talking with friends after the service, the ICU nurse came over and sat next to me. She said, "That was the most amazing thing I've ever seen."

Being with the nurse again helped confirm the reality of the experience. We talked for a bit, and I asked, "How is your family member who we prayed for?"

"He's doing well. I'm still concerned, but he seems to be doing okay."

That was the first and only time I saw the nurse at church.

ONE SPRING DAY TWO YEARS AFTER LEAVING THE LAW firm, selling my house, and moving to the Ballard condo, I accompanied Jane Langer, whose husband had died a few months earlier, to a grief support group at the Swedish Health Services hospital. She was unfamiliar with the neighborhood and asked me to show her the way. Walking down a long, stark, white linoleum hallway, we passed a metal sign on an office door that said Spiritual Care. It caught my attention. I had never heard the term "spiritual care" in a hospital or anywhere else.

After dropping off Jane to her grief support group, I strolled past the door again and thought, *I can go in there and find out what spiritual care is or go home.* The light was on, so I knocked, stepped in, and talked for nearly an hour with a woman who identified herself as a chaplain. She shared with me what chaplains do and all about clinical pastoral education (CPE), a two-year training program to become one. After our conversation, I knew that chaplaincy was the "God job" I had been looking for.

A week later, I learned that the CPE program was being offered at Good Samaritan Hospital in Puyallup in September. It was August when I applied and was accepted.

During the CPE program, I was one of six chaplain interns assigned to a pastor supervisor named Greg. One morning, two women from the Life Center Northwest organ and tissue donor program came to talk to us interns about how the program functioned. It was our job as chaplains to introduce the subject of tissue donation to families whose loved ones had just died in the hospital. The ladies passed around photographs of actual skin and bones to show us what tissues were taken from the body after death and how and when they took them.

The unexpected images horrified me. I thought I had processed grief, making peace with the fact that Ashley's soul lived on. I believed that the soul of a person was the essence and that the body was simply a container. The images caused me to confront for the first time the truth that Ashley's body had died and that the body was integral to a person's essence, not secondary. I felt panicked that parts of her were in pieces far away in India.

Though hanging on with all my might to control my desperation, I felt like I might explode. I managed to not run out of the room. I held my feelings in until the following week. We had a brief check-in with Greg and our group of six interns. Greg listened and provided honest, loving feedback to the interns after their encounters with patients. When it was my turn, much to my horror, I exploded in front of the group. Anguish and terror came gushing out like a monsoon. The room went black. I could no longer see the faces of the other interns. I saw light on Greg's face that accompanied me as I pictured Ashley rushing past me on the river. Sobbing, I reached out, helplessly straining to reach her but unable to catch her.

Greg asked as I reached out, "What color is the water?"

I wondered why he asked and said, "I'm not sure." *Why did he ask me that?*

He asked me that same question at subsequent meetings. I thought it was a trivial question. Who cared what color the water was? It appeared black.

Eventually, MultiCare Healthcare System hired me to be a chaplain, and I worked at several of their health centers,

Firefly

including Tacoma General Hospital, Good Samaritan Hospital in Puyallup, and MultiCare Regional Cancer Center in Auburn.

For twenty-three years, one year more than Ashley's age when she died, I had talked to her every day. Looking at the big picture hanging in my bedroom began to make me uncomfortable. For at least the third time, I told her, "I'm letting you go. You don't need to hang out here with me all the time or keep taking care of me. You're free to go."

When I moved to an apartment a block down the street a few months later, I knew what to do. The photograph needed to fly to Nancy. I took it to UPS where they wrapped it in plastic and brown paper for the flight to Moss Landing, California, where Nancy lived since her return to the United States after successive international positions through her work with CEDPA. It cost a small fortune ($150) to mail, but I was resolved that it was time for Ashley to move on.

I told her, "I'm cutting you down to size." I replaced the memorial poster with a 3x5 photo of her walking out our peach-colored front door at Green Lake in a silver Nepali frame that Nancy sent me years ago. I placed the new framed photo next to an 8x10 of Anna and told Ashley, "When I start talking to you, I'm going to make myself stop. I'll make exceptions on birthdays and holidays. You're free to go now and do your work. Sorry I kept you so long. I hope you'll stop in from time to time though." As I said this, chuckling and talking out loud, I imagined she would think it was as funny as I thought it was. I got a big kick out of the whole thing.

About a week later, I became sad and continually sadder each day, afraid I was going into a depression. I rode it out and emerged in about three weeks. I think it was a real goodbye. At least it was another one.

IN 2020, I BEGAN MEETING WITH ONE OF MY PROFESSORS from Seattle University who was a spiritual director. Spiritual direction is the practice of being with someone and attempting to deepen one's relationship with the divine and grow in personal spirituality. In our first session, I told her of Ashley's distressing dream about endlessly digging in dirt, her becoming utterly exhausted, drained of energy, unimaginably fatigued. As soon as the words came out of my mouth, I realized that torrential rain causes rivers to overflow, resulting in mudslides. People who die in flash floods are buried in mud. It was incredibly strange after twenty-five years to make that connection.

About a week before our meeting, I saw a story on television about a flash flood in India and watched as the land washed away and slid into the river. I confronted the reality that though drowned in water, Ashley was buried in mud.

Denial can be a friend when one is not ready to absorb the truth. Denial for twenty-five years. Buried in mud after drowning in water. It began to make sense why my CPE instructor asked me what color the water was when I had the meltdown in class. I remembered how Ashley insisted that I not close the lids on her dolls, certain they could not breathe. The next flash of insight was that what I had visualized as a brown digestive tract on Ashley's abdomen, as I said goodbye on the porch the night she left on her trip, was perhaps a muddy river.

For at least two years after her death, there was so much I couldn't explain. I continued experiencing signs. While encountering them, I looked into what others had experienced by way of ringing phones, animals behaving oddly, electronics not working, and water appearing inexplicably as it did the night of Anna's rehearsal dinner. In the first year after Ashley's death, I read a book by James Van Praagh, *Talking to Heaven: A Medium's Message of Life after Death*. It was intriguing but scared me. I read a couple of chapters, put it back on the shelf, and eventually recycled it.

Twenty-five years later, I glimpsed an interview of Van Praagh on the side of the screen while watching something else on YouTube. After clicking it, I learned about his Catholic upbringing including church and school. He had briefly attended seminary. He said his belief in God grew to mean peace and love within and around. After discovering his gift of connecting with the spirit world as a child, he began to work as a medium, protecting his readings first by praying.

I decided to read his book I recycled to the Goodwill twenty five-years ago from beginning to end. Toward the end of the book, Van Praagh talks about ways people who have died typically signal to the living that they still exist. I experienced virtually all of them during the search, throughout the next couple of years, or years later. The experiences included affected electrical levels including lights flickering, the TV turning on and off, radios and clocks turning on and off at different times, a phone ringing with silence on the other end, appliances stopping or starting, and a rainbow arcing 180 degrees directly over the house. There were gifts and material items that appeared—birds, ladybugs, or animals coming near, seeming to speak through other people and appearing in dreams. And ever after…

I thought that once Ashley became an adult, she would be safe and would outlive me, the way children are supposed to outlive their parents. She died when she was twenty-two, and in the twenty-six years since, I still had the questions I had asked since my mother died. Was there life after death? What was real? What about calling, mission, destiny?

Having retired from chaplaincy, as I assembled and edited the writing, it was tnteresting that only after arriving at this point, I finally revisited Van Praagh's book. Surprised to read the list of signs that coincided with my experience, I wondered why after writing about these occurrences with Ashley, I was just now finding out that they were included in a laundry list of typical ways of contact.

After I finished writing this book, a friend of Ashley's sent me *Signs* by Laura Lynne Jackson who, like Van Praagh, had a similar list she called "default signs deceased loved ones send." Jackson's list included, among other things, deer, rainbows, ladybugs, birds, butterflies, and music.

BECAUSE OF THE SPIRITUAL AND EMOTIONAL ENERGY IT took to train and work as a chaplain, I placed the writing about Ashley in a file cabinet for seven years. I thought it might stay in the drawer as a means of processing my grief, but the story continually called to be let out to share.

Going back to my first inquiry into the chaplaincy program, after hearing my story and that we never recovered Ashley's body, the head chaplain exclaimed with deep concern, "Oh dear, that is not natural." I think she meant that without seeing the body, one can never get the necessary closure. I know that is the common belief; however, I was relieved to be spared seeing Ashley dead. I wondered though.

I was recently consoled after hearing a story on the radio: interviews with funeral directors who were doing their jobs during the pandemic, working with families who could not be with, see, or say goodbye to loved ones who died from COVID-19. The families said, "We couldn't have closure." One of the funeral directors said, "Closure is a mirage. We carry the grief for the rest of our lives. It can move you in new ways, new directions."

Returning to my original question, "Is there life after death?" My answer is an unequivocal "Yes." I have finally put that one to rest.

As to whether people's lives are planned or destined, I believe at the very least there is purpose, some kind of unique job we are called to do. In Ashley's case, both she and I were getting glimpses of her path forward in premonitions, dreams, and unexplained experiences during and after her life. None of this makes logical sense, but I could see there were connections. All I can make of it now is that there is a lot more going on beyond what the eye can see.

I'm grateful for the tiny glimpses.

Acknowledgments

Peggy Sturdivant, editor, who from my notes turned straw to gold

Nancy Russell, godmother, who searched

Carol Angel, friend, who encouraged me
to write the story

Cris Benson, career advisor, who prescribed writing fifteen minutes every morning

Greg Nealon, MDiv, Clinical Pastoral Education instructor, who led me through

Michael McCausland, neighbor, who set me straight

and to family and friends whose kindness, generosity, and humor brought me hope

I am forever grateful.

Bibliography

Jackson, Laura Lynne. *Signs: The Secret Language of the Universe.* New York: Dial Press, 2020.

Kubler-Ross, Elisabeth. *Remember the Secret.* Millbrae, CA: Celestial Arts, 1982.

Van Praagh, James. *Talking to Heaven: A Medium's Message of Life After Death.* New York: New American Library, 1999.

Endnotes

1. Albert Schweitzer, *The Spiritual Life* (Boston: Beacon Press, 1947), 102.
2. "Firefly," Elizabeth Madox Roberts, https://discoverpoetry.com/poems/firefly-poems/.
3. Anne Cameron, *Daughters of Copperwoman* (Madeira Park, BC: Harbour Publishing, 2002), 23–33.
4. "Fire-Fly," John B. Tabb, https://discoverpoetry.com/poems/firefly-poems/.
5. Chief Seattle's 1854 Oration, https://suquamish.nsn.us/home/about-us/chief-seattle-speech.
6. *The Crack-Up*, F. Scott Fitzgerald, https://www.goodreads.com/quotes/282743-one-should-be-able-to-see-things.
7. "You Are My Sunshine," Jimmie Davis, https://secondhandsongs.com/artist/16300/all.
8. "Somewhere Out There" from *An American Tail* soundtrack, Linda Ronstadt and James Ingram, https://music.youtube.com/watch?v=5jl8mzCaCr0.
9. Ibid.
10. Lewis Carroll, *Alice's Adventure in Wonderland & Through the Looking Glass*, https://www.goodreads.com/quotes/search.
11. Mary Oliver, *Swan: Poems and Prose Poems* (Boston: Beacon Press, 2010), 37.

12 Catharine Feher-Elston, *Ravensong: A Natural and Fabulous History of Ravens and Crows* (London: Penguin Books Ltd., 1991, 2004).

13 *After Life*, Ricky Gervais, https://www.netflix.com/title/80998491.

14 Henri Nouwen, *Bread for the Journey: A Daybook of Wisdom and Faith* (New York: HarperCollins, 2006).

15 Alex Haley and Malcolm X, *The Autobiography of Malcolm X* (New York: Random House Publishing Group, 1964).

16 Charles van Sandwyk, *Mr. Rabbit's Symphony of Nature and Other Tails* (London: The Folio Society, 2020).

17 Frank Ostaseski, *The Five Invitations* (New York: Flatiron Books, 2017), 104.

18 *The Moth Radio Hour*, August 23, 2021.

Made in United States
Troutdale, OR
09/21/2023

13098350R00089